$ELL
YOUR
$TORY

$ELL
YOUR
$TORY

Brand stories that inspire,
influence and ignite
business success

PAULA SMITH

Acknowledgements

To my darling husband, Darren, who is always by my side, ready for the next adventure.

To my three children, Danny, Sarah, and Chloe. Words cannot express what you mean to me and how special it makes me feel when you are proud of your mum.

To my family, friends, and clients who make my life so amazing.

To the sixteen contributors of this publication who have opened their hearts to share their stories. I thank you so much for trusting me with your brand.

And to Julie, who every step of the way has supported the *Sell Your Story* journey.

"Life is not measured by the number of breaths we take, but by the moments that take our breath away."

Brand Stories

$ELL
YOUR
$TORY

Brand stories that inspire,
influence and ignite
business success

Paula Smith

Introduction

I have always been fascinated by business.

As a child, I was the one volunteering to work in the school tuck shop, the one collecting the door money at the end-of-year disco, or the one collecting bottles to take back for a refund so I could save for things Mum and Dad just couldn't afford or didn't think were a priority. I would spend hours watching the money roll in at the local car wash, always pondering did I want to WASH the cars or would I rather OWN the car wash?

I didn't come from a family of entrepreneurs—far from it. Dad worked at the local refinery and Mum was a stay-at-home mum—a job she took very seriously, and one I didn't really appreciate until I became a mum myself and realised just how much she did for Dad and us kids. Not only did I not come from a family of business owners, I didn't even know anyone who owned a business.

Dad did dabble once in a partnership with the local drive-in movie theatre, and of course I was his assistant, running to the corner store to help hang the upcoming movie posters. I was hugely disappointed when he announced it was too much work and he was giving his share of the business away.

I don't know why my parents were so surprised when I started puppet shows on the front lawn for the kids in the street and charged them each twenty cents for the privilege of watching my homemade puppets and brilliant MC skills. In one weekend I earned nearly enough money to go to the Royal Show with one of my friends. I washed my dad's car for the top up money. That was the weekend I also decided I wanted to own the car wash—I definitely did not want to just work in it.

Throughout high school I was still a girl with an entrepreneurial spark and a passion for big ideas. My favourite subjects were maths, drama, and debating; interesting to look back now at all those things I enjoyed so much. I was also thrilled to be offered the opportunity to MC the school assemblies, and then to represent my school as president of the student council. My first real lessons in leadership came that very year. Some of the decisions I had to make were not popular with my peers and others had me choosing between going to the beach with my friends or attending school P and C meetings.

My family life was very "normal" but money was always tight. While my friends indulged in horseback riding, music, and annual holidays, I was introduced to more cost effective options like netball and the amateur theatre group. In fact, Mum, my sister, and I all joined the local theatre group and although I was one of the youngest members, I learned the art of performance, production, marketing, and of course, how to make each production profitable. It didn't seem like a growth journey at the time but the foundation was being laid for my future entrepreneurial path.

My first jobs out of school were many and varied until at last I confessed to my parents that I hated all the jobs I had been doing, and, though I was only eighteen, I really just wanted to own my own business. So with no money, little education, and only a handful of puppet shows behind me, I started a grooming, deportment, and modelling school for kids in my neighbourhood. This same little business quickly grew into the largest in the state. I loved every part of running a business. I was regularly speaking at events, I was making a difference, and I was finally becoming the confident business woman I aspired to be. I even won a business award for the most innovative enterprise in the region. There was no going back to a real job now.

It was during this time I fell in love with training; I even went back to study and completed a training and development degree. I loved being back in the classroom and continued on after graduating to study business, franchising, and adult education by attending weekend and evening classes. Although I was enjoying my life as a busy wife, mum, and business owner, I knew it was time to move out of my comfort zone and take the business to the next level. Franchising and speaking were my growth strategies. And both worked. My franchise became one of the first businesses to franchise children's after-school activities and it became the largest business of its kind in the country. With the help of an amazing group of franchisees, the business grew fast and we proudly became a trusted and recognised brand. I also had the pleasure now of speaking to thousands of clients and potential clients on a regular basis.

In fact, speaking has enabled me to grow multiple businesses and position myself in a busy marketplace over and over again. And although I sold my franchise group many years ago—and have reaped the rewards from other successful business opportunities—I have never let go of my love for speaking, training, and business.

Today, as a professional speaker, author, and business consultant, I am fortunate enough to work with other entrepreneurs, helping them to grow their businesses and brands. I also work with large organisations, helping their key staff to harness the power of speaking and presenting to build both internal and external relationships.

Thirty years on, I still love what I do. I love the clients I work with and I love to hear about their entrepreneurial journeys; their why stories; their brand stories.

I know from my years of speaking to tens of thousands of audience members in all areas of business it's the stories that connect the best. Stories evoke emotion, stories help us to learn, stories embed in the brain in a completely different way. Nothing is ever as engaging as a great story.

Being on the speaking circuit and listening to hundreds of inspirational stories, as well as working with some awesome clients over the past few years, really fuelled the idea to share their stories in print.

We learn from the wisdom and experiences of others, as well as our own. I hope you enjoy reading the life and business lessons that my contributors are sharing here. I have carefully chosen the contributors of the first Sell Your Story publication.

In the following pages you will get to meet ordinary people creating commercial opportunities by sharing their memories, their experiences, and the lessons they have learned along the way. Through speaking, publishing, business, and philanthropy, these authors are not only creating a business of their dreams; they're contributing to our communities and making a difference. Their stories are their brand.

As I put the finishing touches to this publication, my husband and I, with our smallest child in tow, are about to embark on a year away from Australia to enjoy all Canada has to offer. I hope to meet many more interesting entrepreneurs on my travels and gather many more stories to share with you.

I encourage you to share your brand stories too.

Paula

Colin Hendrie

There's no growth without challenge

*"If it doesn't challenge you,
it doesn't change you."*

— Fred DeVito

Colin grew up in Zimbabwe, first in the city and then later on the family farm. His father ran a successful real estate business that his father before him had run. When Colin was ten years old, tragically his Mother died and not long after, his father's business began to fail. After being forced to liquidate all his assets—including the family farm—Colin's father took up employment as the manager at a large cattle ranch. Sixty-four thousand acres of bush land was now available for Colin to explore whenever he wanted.

Money was tight and due to lack of funding, Colin was not able to go on to college after completing his education, so he joined the army and spent the next eleven years as an infantry officer. The change in government in 1980 and the instability that led to prompted Colin, his wife, and their two young daughters to immigrate to South Africa. Here, Colin worked in various management positions ranging from retail, manufacturing, and car rental. He then joined a partner in manufacturing and installing their own security systems. This went well until one day, Colin got a call from London, asking if he was interested in joining the Sultan of Oman's Special Force as a squadron commander. He joined, despite having little knowledge of what he was in for, and he and his family spent three wonderful years there.

In 1990, Colin and his family immigrated to Australia. It was a move they would not regret. He worked for two years for a group of entrepreneurs in the process control industry, both in Australia and the

United States. Itchy feet, a desire to help others succeed and forty years of leadership experience led Colin to his own entrepreneurial dream. Colin started Outback Initiatives in 1984, a company focusing on group and individual development using experiential learning principles to achieve their clients' goals. Sharing the experiences of ex-Rhodesian army officer and Omani Special Forces squadron commander, and the exploration lessons from living on sixty-four thousand acres sets the scene for any leadership challenge.

Have you always wanted to own your own business?

I grew up in a family where my father had owned his own business and got the bug then to do my own thing. While I have worked for other people and organisations, I always got frustrated with the fear of those organisations' reluctance to innovate. I could never understand why organisation would not move into unchartered territory. I also got itchy feet once I had become comfortable in my role within that organisation.

I recall coming home to my family one day and advising them that I had resigned from my job and did not have any idea what I was going to do, other than I would be doing something on my own. At the time, I was very comfortable in my role as sales director of a national car rental company. I knew I had the passion and self-belief; it was just a matter of finding an opportunity that interested me and where I felt I had the skills and experience to make a success of it. An opportunity arose when a start-up company in security alarm systems was looking for franchise operators. I arranged an interview with the owner and left the meeting as an equal shareholder after having sold a business plan on a flipchart in the owner's office. The company grew very quickly and successfully but regrettably I emigrated before I could contribute to further growth.

How critical is it to have a team support you?

Keeping your staff motivated and committed to the company is essential. When they feel they play a meaningful part in the organisation, they go that 'extra mile' without hesitation. This enables the directors to focus on the business and not be preoccupied with staff issues which can become very time-consuming. Letting go and allowing them the freedom to make decisions in their area of responsibility is also important.

Recognising one's own strengths and weaknesses is also essential. Filling the areas of weakness with somebody who has the skills creates a 'win-win' for the organisation. After being a sole director in Outback Initiatives for the first ten years, I realised the organisation had grown where I desperately needed support in finance and administration. Fortuitously, I met up with Sheryll Fisher whom I had previously worked with in the United States, and while she had little understanding of experiential learning, I knew she had the desire and commitment and excellent skills to support me. I offered her 50% of the company and after a day she accepted. A big risk for her since she had teenage children to support as a single mother, but today she makes a significant contribution in all those areas mentioned, and additionally now takes the lead role in the company. Without her support, Outback Initiatives would not have grown to where it is today and have a product that we feel is unequalled in the niche market that we operate in.

> *"Having a committed team behind you allows you to focus on the key objectives of the company."*

How important is innovation in business?

When the business is operating successfully there is often a degree of complacency that goes with it. The question becomes: why tamper with something that works well, especially when clients continually show complete satisfaction with the program outcomes?

We have always been open to trying new initiatives despite the concerns that these initiatives may not work. When we compare today's products with those say, ten years ago, the basic principles of experiential learning are there but there are now several enhancements that make it more effective and professional.

In our industry, it is not difficult for competitors to hear about new innovations introduced by us, and to adopt them under the mask of a different name. It is difficult to protect them as your intellectual property, so we have taken the view that as long as we keep enhancing our product, we will stay a step ahead of the opposition.

How do you juggle your work/life balance?

For the majority of my working life I have spent long periods of time away from home and the family. During the latter part of my military career in the Rhodesian Army, I was deployed on operations for six-week periods followed by ten days 'rest and recuperation'. I had two young daughters at the time and after getting back home after a six-week period my daughters felt I was a stranger for the first couple of days and then we were very close. I recall them clinging to the vehicle when my driver arrived to pick me up to go away again, which was heartbreaking. I realised then the effect long absences had on my family. I made sure my family was able to join me, during my stint with the Sultan's Special Force of Oman. And as it turned out, it was a great adventure for us all.

When planning Outback Initiatives, the business model meant that one third of my time would be away running programs, one third recovery time, and one third doing program preparation from home. While the one third away was not desirable for the family, it was necessary for the financial side of the business because time away equals revenue. With the generous time at home doing part preparation, part working and part downtime, I manage now to achieve a great work/life balance. A strategy that I believe should be factored into any business planning.

> *"Do your homework on the market."*

Why do you think many small businesses fail?

I believe there are several key areas to operating a successful business that go hand in hand with each other.

The product must be a winner. It must be relevant to the marketplace and have some key areas to entice would-be users. It is important that you also know which key areas are relevant to each client, as they differ. Before approaching a prospective client, find out what they really want and present a case tailored to that.

Do your homework on the market. Developing a product in an existing market is much less financially sapping than trying to develop a new market. I do not believe that venturing into unknown territory is not worthwhile; however, you should be certain you have the resources to allow for a concerted effort in this regard.

Your business plan must be realistic and cover the following:

o   Can you realistically get enough of the market to be viable?

o   Are the product margins sufficient to get profitability?

o   Do you have the people and financial resources to sustain a reasonable start-up period?

o   What differentiates your product from those of your competitors?

o   Keep it simple. Focus on the key areas and don't be sidetracked by opportunities that are not in line with the business plan.

o   Do not take on business that is not profitable. Occasionally there may be the temptation to take on break-even opportunities or even those which may create a small loss in favour of turnover.

o   If you have a passion about your business or product, it will keep your intensity and focus.

What do you believe holds people back from achieving their dream business or life?

Since our business is about people and organisations developing their potential to be more successful, we frequently see evidence of those barriers to achieving full potential. The first and perhaps the most common area is lack of self-belief. Many individuals fail to see the potential they have and are reluctant to take a risk and attempt something different. It often takes the feedback from others to convince them that they have the potential. Getting them to observe others who appear to have the same potential but have taken the step to do bigger and greater things often is the catalyst to change.

The perceived need for job or financial security influences their mind that it will be unsafe to venture into foreign territory. Sometimes this is the excuse to defer the idea of embarking on a new journey because there is no guarantee to being successful. I believe there are countless individuals who do not enjoy their current employment, and are often under immense pressure in one way or another. When you consider that one probably spends in excess of fifty percent of one's working life either at work or thinking about work, surely you owe it to yourself to get out of the rut and do something different.

It took me several years to embark on something that I had a passion for, rather than something that paid well. I took all thoughts of the secure options for employment and said to myself, 'Without thinking of job or financial security, what would you most like to do?' That immediately reduced the list to two, one of which was not possible. The other was adopted and I can honestly say that every day for the last twenty-two years I enjoy rising early and getting into my work.

Did you have any formal qualifications to go into your business?

While there are no mandatory qualifications to do human resource development in an experiential way such as we do, there are obviously some skills that I consider essential.

Most important is life skills. My working life has been a combination of military in two armies, commercial experience at a senior level on several continents, and embarking on two successful new business enterprises. Added to this was an eventful upbringing in rural Zimbabwe (Rhodesia). These life skills have enabled me to gain the confidence and respect of participants on our programs, particularly where we are involving them in uniquely designed activities that are often high perceived risk activities, but low actual risk activities.

We deal with a wide range of clients in all sorts of industries, and it would be impossible to be an expert in all of those fields. Fortunately, when facilitating groups in an experiential context, it is the people aspects that we are focussing on and not the technical side of their businesses. We facilitate them in such a way that they determine their journey and the realisations that go with it. I recall facilitating a very senior group of directors and managers in the mining industry when I first engaged in the facilitation field, and after the ten-day program, I felt that I had perhaps not engaged enough with the group. However, the feedback I received was very complimentary, particularly that I gave the group the freedom to steer their own ship, so to speak. Clearly, they were not aware of my inner lack of confidence. The learning from that program gave me the confidence to be more relaxed with senior groups of people and also that I had no need to control the group's thinking or actions but simply to keep them focused on the key people issues. The less interference from me the better.

A lot of our focus in the business is developing business leaders at various levels. While it may be advantageous to have a relevant qualification in business management or leadership, there is no substitute for having real life experiences and opportunities leading people in all sorts of environments.

What have been some of your most difficult challenges in your business?

Our growth has been mainly through existing clients or associates, principally because they know how effective our programs have been. While we are aware of that and continue to market through them, it is always a challenge to effectively engage new clients who have no knowledge of us and what we have to offer.

Articulating what we do to clients so they fully understand what we are about has also been a challenge. Because we do most of our experiential work in the outdoors, we are often perceived as operators in the adventure industry. We offer our clients many unusual activities that have an adventurous component, but they are a means to an end. It is about how they tackle the task and not the task itself. We also have the Gurkha Contingent of The Singapore Police, who have been a client for over twenty years and their program is a little different to our normal corporate client programs.

Our corporate market is something of a niche market in that it is sometimes difficult to get financial commitment into an unknown area and can be difficult to measure the results. In some cases, it could be the lack of a formal certificate which is the issue. The most effective tool to sway their commitment is the use of referrals and the results we achieve.

Colin Hendrie
www.outbackin.com.au

Darren Vernede

Resilient People Beat Impossible Odds

"I think everyone should go to college and get a degree and then spend six months as a bartender and six months as a cabdriver. Then they would really be educated."

-Al McGuire

Let's calculate the odds of surviving to manhood, enjoying a wonderful marriage, and fathering three perfectly healthy, robust children. For most the odds are in their favour but for a fellow born with haemophilia then affected by HIV/AIDS and then diagnosed with the potentially deadly Hepatitis C virus.

The odds are *incalculable*.

Yet one man *has* survived and is part of a thriving family despite those odds. Darren Vernede believes, to the core of his being, that the reason he's still here is because he's "almost ridiculously resilient."

What *is* resiliency? Positive thinking? Decisiveness? Situational strategies? Something else? *All of the above?*

With more than two decades as an executive coach, speaker, and real life, in-the-trenches business executive, Darren's viewpoint on resilience is radically different than most other professionals.

Alternately called a 'Passionate Provocateur' and a 'People Whisperer' because of his ability to stir up groups and bring out the best in each of them, Darren is renowned for his practical, street-savvy style, his infusion of real-life stories, and the way he connects conversationally on intimate, intense, and individual levels.

Darren's book 'Resilience: Bouncing Back from the Edge of Death' shares the details of his multiple early brushes with the fate and his relentless refusal to accept it. Being infected with HIV after a tainted blood tranfusion during a routine medical treatment that Darren had endured most of his life would be the catalyst for many to just give up. Darren has managed to not only stay positive but has also been proactive against accumulating odds as the years have passed.

An inspiration to anyone who is facing challenges with enormous odds, Darren's life story is sure to resonate with business owners, entrepreneurs, and people facing life-threatening illnesses. His first book is a must-read for teenagers in middle- and high school and young adults who may be considering their present challenges insurmountable.

Resilience is attainable. Darren shows people how to find it within themselves and how to use it to achieve their own "impossible" dreams.

Did you come from a family of entrepreneurs?

The short answer to this is no, although my father had an entrepreneurial spirit.

He would work sometimes three jobs at a time to support our family when we were young children as our medical costs and normal daily living costs were such that a single income stream wasn't enough. He would work the traditional 9 to 5 JOB but in the evenings he would sell encyclopedias for a company. I guess it was the early MLM style marketing system. Dad would also work on the weekends selling products for another company which was homewares and cleaning products.

In later years, when I was old enough, Dad would teach me the art of sales and customer service by setting up a mobile video business in the early 1980s, back in the VHS video tape days. It seems almost prehistoric thinking about it now, but the world was a different place such a short time ago. We provided a mobile video library for people living in outer suburban areas who would normally have to travel more than fifteen or twenty kilometers to the nearest shop. We did well for a number of years and had multiple buses on the road at the height of the business, but the suburbs moved further out and eventually the business became a sunset business, and, with the increase of video shop chains it became less viable to operate.

I learned several valuable lessons in those years. One would be always keep an eye on new trends and shifts in business, and to evolve your business to suit the times—never be satisfied with the status quo.

The following quote sums up what I am eluding to in my answer:

> *"There are no secrets to success.*
> *It is the result of preparation, hard work,*
> *and learning from failure."*
>
> Colin Powell

What advice would you give to someone thinking about starting their own business?

Know your why first: Why do you want to get into business, what is your passion?

The key to starting and running your own business is answering that question first; otherwise you are just buying yourself a JOB.

Is your reason for lifestyle? That will direct you to a business you can earn good money with limited time input or a business which is easily run from a laptop or other technology. If your passion is for customer interaction or an enjoyment of a particular skill, that will guide you to a different business structure.

If you know your *why* and *what* your passion is, then that will guide you to selecting the right business model and type of business to get into. If your passion is haircutting and you build a business around selling hair products, then you may be successful but you will never feel fulfilled and you will become bored and frustrated in your business. You should have set up a salon business and built it into a chain of salons which promotes your personal flair and style of haircutting.

The second piece of advice would be to not rush anything. Research your market and your competition in the marketplace; never build a business soley on being the cheapest in town. Always be the best in your chosen market and gain the necessary skills required to position yourself as the expert in your field. Anyone can do cheap and you will always be at the mercy of the new up and comer who can undercut you by five percent. It's a war of attrition rather than one of skill.

The last piece of advice would be always keep learning and evolving in your business. Never be sitting on past successes or accolades, keep striving to become better at what you do and stay one step ahead of your competition.

Do you think it's important to have a mentor?

Yes, I believe that you absolutely need to look for someone who has achieved similar business goals for which you are aspiring to.

It's a very important part of setting up and running a successful business to have someone who has gone through many of the trials and tribulations of being in business. Sometimes they can save you a lot of heartache and money, especially in the early phases.

> *"Your work is going to fill a large part of your life,*
> *and the only way to be truly satisfied is to do*
> *what you believe is great work. And the only*
> *way to do great work is to love what you do.*
> *If you haven't found it yet, keep looking.*
> *Don't settle. As with all matters of the*
> *heart, you'll know when you find it."*
>
> Steve Jobs

It is important that you find the right mentor. They don't have to necessarily be in the same type of business but as long as they have had a lot of experience in running a successful business and they click with you on a personal level then they can offer you some insights to time management, budget setting, and general management skills.

I personally have had several mentors over the years and each one has brought me a sense of not being alone and that if they can do it, then so can I. I have set up and run several businesses over the years. My first business was in computer repairs, which was successful in the early 1990s. I had a mentor working with me in that venture. My second business was in electronics retail and I had two mentors during the five years I ran that business. My third business was in wholesale importing and was a very tough business to be in, with many ways to lose money quickly if you made a wrong purchase at the wrong time, and I was very lucky to have a brilliant semi-retired ex-importer as a mentor; he saved the shirt on my back many times.

In my current business I have a mentor who has given me many insights into shortcomings that I never knew I had. I felt I was a great presenter and had excellent business skills, as I had been successful over many businesses and many years, but she has shone a light into some areas of myself I hadn't explored because I had become complacent.

A good mentor is a wise investment in your business as they can help give you peace of mind and a shoulder to cry on if all goes pear shaped.

> "I've seen that phenomenally successful people believe they can learn something from everybody. I call them 'mavericks with mentors.' Surround yourself with incredibly successful, smart people and listen to them."

Do you set regular goals?

Absolutely yes, goals are a roadmap for success. Without something to strive for then you just wander aimlessly through life as well as business.

When I was first diagnosed with HIV, the one thing that I believe kept me on course was the goals I set for myself every year. Instead of making a new year's resolution, which nobody truly keeps, I sat down by myself and projected forward twelve months and would set small milestones for each quarter, like finish reading a book or live to see an event which was coming up and then see myself actually in the moment at that event.

I wanted to travel so I set a goal one year to take a few months off of work and go to the USA and travel the Route 66. I set that goal for 1993, and in November of 1993 I made it happen. My goal kept me on track and kept my focus on a bigger picture rather than the crisis of health I was going through at the time. The time that focus brought me meant that the new drugs which were being developed in 1989 and 1990 became availble to me and brought me back from the brink of death.

Goal setting is also vitally important in business as it brings a focus of where you are heading in your business. You absolutely need to do regular checks on your goals to see if they are still relevant to your business or life.

So set a goal but also don't be so rigid that you are not able to adjust it to the changing scene, which in business can be ever-changing as with life. Crises can change the original goal so adjust it to suit but still keep in mind the original goal and work your way back to it when the situation allows.

> "Set a goal but also don't be so rigid that you are not able to adjust it to the changing scene."

> *"It's not an accident that musicians become musicians and engineers become engineers: it's what they're born to do. If you can tune into your purpose and really align with it, setting goals so that your vision is an expression of that purpose, then life flows much more easily."*
>
> Jack Canfield

What type of education do you value?

This is a bit of a tough question. I personally belive a lot more can be learned from the school of hard knocks; in other words, doing the work in the trenches and learning from your mistakes.

The caveat I would put on my statement would be that if you are going to be a brain surgeon then I would prefer you had many years of university education first and then many more years as an intern learning the practical hands-on part of the job under a brilliant older surgeon, especially if it was my brain you would be working on!

Education comes in many forms and really, it depends on your particular chosen business path.

I was working towards becoming a medical doctor before my diagnosis of HIV so I do have qualifications in that area, but they are not relevant to my current or past businesses. Almost all of my education in my current business comprises of the degree of school of hard knocks, but I am constantly learning new skills and applying them to my business. I have recently begun podcasting and interviewing people who have been through life-changing events in an attempt to broaden my knowledge base of what it means to be resilient and how that differs from one person to another, and one challenge to another.

Education in whatever form is very important in your personal and business life, as with knowledge comes power. When you know something and understand it then you can master it and leverage that into more income and a better lifestyle.

Is failure part of learning in business?

Failure is part of life in general. The only person who has never experienced failure is a person who has never done or achieved anything in their life. Sometimes failure can be the best teacher. The process of failing at something comes with an emotional, physical, and mental strain which reinforces a lesson that is always remembered.

I have made many mistakes and had many failures throughout my life. Everytime I come through a failure, I try to look for the reason for the failure and how I can possibly avoid making the same errors again.

An important lesson for me was to never be completely comfortable in your business. By that I mean don't become complacent, always keep an eye on evolving trends in your market and move with them. Don't allow your business to become a sunset business, or, if it is enevitable, then make changes to your business or structure to move into a similar emerging market.

> *"It is impossible to live without failing at something,*
> *unless you live so cautiously that you might*
> *has well not have lived at all, in which*
> *case you have failed by default."*
>
> J. K. Rowling

How important is resilience for success?

Resilience is what I do, so I would say that this would be probably the most important asset an entrepreneur or business owner would need to have in their personal skill set.

In business as in life, there are many situations which can be life- (or business) threatening: accidents, injuries, loss of clients, downturn in markets etc. All these crisis events can happen at any time and how you deal and react to the crisis will determine your future directions in life or business.

Resilience is the ability to pick yourself up and dust yourself off after a major crisis and to find a positive outcome, to learn a lesson, or to simply survive and live the best quality life you can after the event.

Resilience is the ability to know that the crisis you are facing is purely transient and temporary, its time will pass life will continue whether you get up and keep going or simply stay down and wallow in self pity. Resilience is to keep getting up after every punch or kick life throws at you and keep moving forward, even if it is in a different direction than you were heading.

As I say all the time, the human organism is, by default, resilient. No human infant would ever learn to crawl, stand, balance, walk, run, play, study or work without resiliency.

Most of us are *always* 'failing forward.' It's the people who think there's no point in trying who begin to lose traction and hope and eventually surrender to whatever fate lies ahead.

Resiliency is *'Oh, yes, we can!" and 'Oh, yes, we will!'* Resiliency is our inborn *gumption gear*. Without resilience we would never try or do anything. It's just a skill we often lose as we get older and more world weary, but with all things, if you exercise the resilience muscle, often you get stronger and more resilient.

> *"Because, you know, resilience—if you think*
> *of it in terms of the Gold Rush—then you'd*
> *be pretty depressed right now because the*
> *last nugget of gold would be gone.*
> *But the good thing is, with innovation,*
> *there isn't a last nugget. Every new thing*
> *creates two new questions and*
> *two new opportunities."*
>
> Jeff Bezos

What have been some of your most difficult challenges in business?

One of my biggest challenges both personally and in business was that I always became wound up in the need to be perfect in anything I produced. The fact is that life itself isn't perfect and if you are always looking to be perfect you never finish anything.

My book was nearly ten years in the writing because I would start writing and then stop after a chapter or two, as I always thought it wasn't good enough or compelling enough that anyone would ever be interested in reading my boring story. I was finally kicked in the pants by my mentor who last year opened my eyes to what I had been doing, which was self sabotaging my success. I just had to sit down and write the bloody thing to completion.

I suddenly found myself writing 3000 to 4000 words a day and within two months my book was complete and in print. I am now in the process of researching for another book which is to be a historical overview of haemophilia, HIV, and hepatitis C, and the human stories that are part of that history, including my own.

The key message from this is to always put out your best work but don't get bogged down in aiming to get it perfect the first time; as long as you put your best efforts into anything then you can always improve on the next version.

Perfection is an unattainable goal.

Just get started and enjoy the ride.

Darren Vernede
www.positivelifecoach.solutions

Gen George

Disrupting the employment industry

"Better to be 80% ready and in the race, than 100% ready and have missed it altogether."

Phil George

Gen George
is the twenty-four-year old founder and CEO of One-Shift, an online jobs platform that operates like a matchmaking service for employers and jobseekers looking for casual, part-time, and full-time employment across a range of industries. Launched in 2012 when Gen was just twenty-one years old, the platform now caters to more than 400,000 jobseekers and 36,000 businesses.

The idea for OneShift came when Gen deferred her Property Law scholarship to embark on a gap year in Europe. She tried to secure casual work to support her travels but found the process to be a night-mare. Discovering that her friends abroad were having similar problems securing work that fit around their schedules, Gen realised there was an obvious gap in the market for flexible work opportunities both at home and globally. She founded OneShift as the solution.

Since its launch, OneShift has grown from a team of one with a sticky-taped WordPress site, to a team of forty with a significant user-base and an Android and iOS app. It has also received a $5 million investment, expanded to New Zealand, and this year acquired mature-age jobs platform Adage. OneShift is proving to be a major disruptor within the recruitment industry, having grown its client roster from small businesses who need a scalable approach to hiring to include major well-known Australian brands.

Gen has been recognised for her achievements with a string of local and global awards and has spoken at a number of events including panel discussions at events hosted by Mashable and General Assembly, presenting at the annual PCO Conference & Exhibition, as well as taking the stage at Google's Sudo event. Others include Girl Geek Sydney's Female Digital Entrepreneur Night and events hosted by Boston Consulting Group, Y Combinator, BBY, KPMG and Ensemble Australia.

Have you always wanted to own your own business?

I did always want to own my business, but more importantly, I just wanted to be able to go to work for something that I was passionate and excited about. A lot of people think that owning your business can result in a more relaxed life where you're not controlled by someone else's objectives, rules, or even hours. Personally, I was never under any illusions as to what the life of an entrepreneur would be like—tough work, long and unpredictable hours, a lot of mistakes and learning experiences, but also an incredible career that opens me up to so many inspiring people and innovative ideas that I might never have been exposed to otherwise.

People who start their own businesses generally have to be people that don't want to wait around for others to solve problems. I've always had a bit of an entrepreneurial streak. My siblings and I never really received an allowance, so I was always motivated to work hard and earn my own money. In high school, I set up my own babysitting club—it was the best way for me and my friends to earn some cash while keeping our schedules flexible. Looking back, this is probably what got me started on my path to creating OneShift. A few years later, when I was twenty-one, I was halfway through my Property Law degree and decided to take a gap year and travel through Europe. I wanted to find casual work overseas to support myself as I travelled, but found this to be so difficult. The people I met overseas were having the same problems, so I decided that when I returned home to Australia I'd get started on a simple, cost-effective solution for people who wanted to work, but needed flexible options. OneShift came out of my own frustrations with the current recruitment system both at home and abroad—it was started to solve issues that I'd experienced firsthand.

> *"People who start their own businesses generally have to be people that don't want to wait around for others to solve problems."*

Do you think it is important to have hobbies or interests outside of business?

I think it's absolutely essential to have hobbies and interests outside of business. I know the expression goes that if you love what you do, you'll never work a day in your life, but sometimes you still need to step outside the office for some fun. It's not just about keeping up your old activities either—although that's important—it's about making sure that you keep looking for new activities and ways to meet new people.

Sometimes when you're stressed out or work is super busy, it can be tempting to retreat from everything else in order to focus, but it's actually allowing yourself time to think, be creative, talk to friends, or even exercise, that can give you the energy you need to deliver the results your business and your team need. Hobbies can expose you to totally new environments and viewpoints that you have never considered before. This can sometimes give the best workarounds or solutions for problems in your own business.

How do you stay inspired and motivated?

I stay inspired and motivated by surrounding myself with other entrepreneurs and business owners who are driving innovation in their industries. Networking events are a great way to do this. I've also been lucky enough to be involved in speaking panels and events where I not only get to interact and develop relationships with some incredible people, but I also get to speak to aspiring entrepreneurs. In particular, I love being part of the great women entrepreneurs community that is so supportive here in Australia. I've made some great friends through these networks and connecting with these creative minds is a huge motivation for me to keep going.

I also try to make sure that I'm connecting with my own customers and clients regularly so as not to lose touch with the whole reason I started OneShift. Hearing from people who are loving their new jobs, or who have found a wonderful worker to join their team through our service, is always a great feeling. At the same time, talking to customers about any concerns they may have and listening to feedback is crucial to driving the business forward. When I was younger I used to go to work with my dad. I thought I was 'helping' in the coleslaw production line and 'helping' pack apple bags but I am pretty sure I created more work than I completed. But, what I did learn from my dad was the importance of being on the factory ground speaking to everyone on the team about what is working, what is not working, and what their thoughts are on fixing it. This made everyone

> "*Listening to feedback is crucial to driving the business forward.*"

feel involved, valued, and created a great place for people to want to come and work.

How do you juggle your work/life balance?

Work/life balance is the foundation of my business, not just something I try to achieve in my own life. OneShift is all about enabling a 'work to live' attitude rather than a 'live to work' attitude, by encouraging more flexibility in the workplace. It's something that is becoming more important to jobseekers and more acceptable to employers.

Even in my own business, I understand that some of our site developers find it more useful to work on the site in the evenings, so for them, a 9-5 job just isn't practical. Allowing people to work from home when it's possible and to navigate their own hours to a certain extent can go a long way to creating a happy and productive workplace. I actually prefer to start my day early by getting in an hour before most of the team arrives, as it lets me get all those little admin tasks out of the way and also means that I'm not staying late in the evening to tie up loose ends. I like to schedule any of my planned catch-ups with my friends and family into my calendar. It just makes sure that I'm reminded throughout the day and don't end up putting things off because I'm too stuck into work.

What are you most proud of in your business?

The thing I'm most proud of in my business is my team. Having seen OneShift grow from just me and a WordPress site to a team of more than forty is a pretty great feeling. We're a tight-knit group of people with so many different interests, skills, and experiences but we're all committed and passionate about what we're doing. It's a pleasure to come to work each day. A core goal as a CEO has been to keep that fun and exciting culture alive, even as our team and customer base grows.

On a different note, I'm also proud of our contribution to the wider conversation about flexibility in the workforce and its growing importance, not just for the younger generation but also for mature age workers. It's something that I've been very vocal about over the years and it's a key philosophy behind the business. It's great to see other players in the industry pushing for the same kind of attitude change and to be a part of that.

Is speaking a part of your marketing strategy?

Speaking is definitely a big part of building my own profile in the business, entrepreneur, and tech communities, but it's also a great way to network and to engage with like-minded people. I choose to speak at events for a variety of reasons depending on the audience and the topic. Opportunities like Google Sudo, where I presented to a room of aspiring entrepreneurs, allow me to share my own mistakes and achievements with those who can learn from them. On the other hand, if I'm looking to increase clients within a certain industry, then I have pursued opportunities that allow me to reach those groups. I also love being part of a panel where I can actually engage with other business owners or entrepreneurs who have come together to discuss an issue that's important to us.

What does a typical day look like to you?

I start off each day having breakfast with my father. We talk strategy, but also get to catch up and share what else is happening in our lives. I get up early so that I can be one of the first people in the office. It just gives me that extra hour or two to clear my inbox and attend to any outstanding tasks from the evening before. If it is a Monday, we have our 2IC team meeting catch-ups, or Tuesday Management meetings to go over what is happening in each department. What is great about One-Shift is the ability to all get pulled into a room randomly, flesh out an idea, and adapt to what results or new data we are receiving. It means we are able to create a nimble and fluid business that can get the best results. I generally also see a couple of clients and suppliers. Evenings are for industry events and catching up on emails.

What have been some of your most difficult challenges in business?

One of the biggest challenges in running my own business has been learning to question everything. I'm a big believer in talking things through with others and seeking out advice from my mentors or those who have had more experience. At the same time, it's important not to just immediately accept what you're being advised to do. Seek out a variety of opinions so you know you have considered it from every angle, but also do your own independent research and talk your findings through with relevant members of your team. If you're running your own business, it's not an option to just accept the status quo. Question everything, every day, and encourage your team to ask questions as well.

Gen George
www.oneshift.com

Gillian Skeer

The Change Agent

*Every day, in every way, we have
the potential for change*

"Four laws of happiness:

*1.Count your blessings,
2. Proclaim your rarity,
3. Go another mile,
4. Use wisely your power of choice."*

Og Mandino, *The Greatest Miracle in the World*

From an early age, Gillian Skeer embraced the concept of change and saw the potential in looking at things differently. She loved self-improvement, and knew that she wanted to be the best person she could be, at the same time making a greater difference. She was a high-achiever and quickly developed her aspiration for self-improvement and experiential growth, through education and extensive world travel. Inspired by some early words of wisdom from her dad—'Gill, you've got the ball at your feet, all you have to do is kick it,'— Gillian has continued to be fueled by opportunities for her own growth, and the growth she can bring about in others.

Gillian Skeer is *The Change Agent*. She is a professional Life & Success Master Coach, life transition specialist, motivator, instructor, columnist, author, and speaker. She is passionately committed to helping her clients achieve their full potential in every aspect of their lives: career and business, personal, mindset and performance, health, relationships, and finances. Gillian connects people with their inherent abilities and strengths to bring about incredible results in their lives.

With over 25 years' experience in an extensive range of professional roles, including coaching, public relations, events management, corporate sponsorship, fundraising, sales, organisational change, business development, and marketing, she is dedicated to delivering specialist expertise and quality client service.

Gillian has applied her skills in a number of industries including retail, property, banking, luxury goods, mining, education, conservation, and tourism; in private, government, and not-for-profit sectors, and has also operated several of her own businesses. Her brand development initiatives have been implemented with organisations such as world-leading diamond producer, Argyle Diamonds, and globally recognised wildlife conservation agency, Perth Zoo.

Training and development under the world's greats have fashioned Gillian's innate skills for facilitating remarkable change. Gillian has established her own life and success coaching company, Creative Coaching Solutions. As *The Change Agent*, Gillian has written for several publications and authored her own column with Fairfax Media on-line news sites.

As well as contributing to *Sell Your Story*, Gillian is a co-author of the books *Millionaire Coach* and *The Inspiration Bible*.

Tell us about yourself and your brand.

I'm a Master Life and Success Coach, branded as *The Change Agent*. My role, and my privilege, is to enable others to reach their full potential through empowering change.

Armed with world-class qualifications and vast experience from many professional roles, I attract clients who are seeking peak performance and outstanding results for their lives.

I'm passionate about what I do; it's my calling. I am fortunate to work with the most amazing people. I help my clients move from where they are in life to where they want to be, to live the life they want to live. I help them become resourceful so that they can be fully equipped and empowered to live an extraordinary life.

My story is about working hard, passion, personal and professional development, consistency of effort, trying new things, working hard, connecting with people, high-standards, excellent service, building my brand, and did I mention working hard? But that's me. I give it my all. And, I am rewarded tenfold.

> *"My mission is to inspire, motivate, and empower people to their better future."*

The awesome thing is, that through all my amazing successes, as well as all the tough encounters in life, I have found a greater understanding of what it means to be human, to be real, to be and do the best I can, to face the types of challenges my clients face, and therefore be better-equipped to support them.

Despite the challenges that we've all had to face in life, and despite where various roads may have taken us, our experiences forge us into our next level of greatness. We all have the potential for change, in all we do, every day.

I've come to understand my greatest strengths, values, passions, skills, and the things that stir my soul, and that is what I want for my clients.

I believe in professionalism, optimum care, leadership, authenticity, warmth and fun, attention-to-detail, excellent customer service, and the advancement of purposeful momentum towards successful outcomes.

Whether through my writing, professional speaking, one-to-one coaching, group workshops, my online presence, or my products, my mission is to inspire, motivate, and empower people to their better future, to provide a forum for them to connect with their inherent strengths, to gain clarity and meaning, to develop congruency with who they are and how they live, to develop an unwavering belief in themselves, and to be charged with a sense of purpose and momentum towards their compelling future.

Real and sustainable change is possible.

What do you believe holds people back from achieving their dream business or life?

Most of the things that hold people back from achieving usually start with their thinking: Lack of belief in themselves, fear of failure, assuming they have to know it all before they start a new project.

It really is all in the thinking. I work with many clients who dream of getting into business for themselves, or want to take their business to the next level. But they often fail to take the first step, or they readily give up. The root cause of what holds them back is their thinking.

What you believe to be true about yourself or about your ability to succeed, all starts with your thinking. What you think directly affects your reality. If you are thinking you might fail, then that's your reality. If you are thinking you don't have enough resources, knowledge, experience, or are not good enough, then that's your reality.

"*Real and sustainable change is possible.*"

These beliefs are limiting. And limiting beliefs are simply things you believe to be true about yourself, which, in reality, are possibly not true. You have just decided to believe them to be true. These beliefs can become patterns of thinking that keep us from changing and thereby, achieving success. They become an entrenched belief, when we run those patterns of thinking over and over again. In other words, a habit.

Giving power to your limiting beliefs will limit your potential, your opportunities, your level of satisfaction and your success.

I've helped many, many people to overcome the limiting beliefs that have held them captive. I've helped them become resourceful so that they can be fully equipped and empowered to live an extraordinary life.

Change your story, change the dialogue that runs through your mind; utilise encouraging, determined, and purposeful thinking and take positive action—this will radically change your outcomes, bringing you closer to the future you desire.

> *"You can if you think you can."*
>
> Norman Vincent Peale

What is your favourite quote that you live by?

There are many quotes I love but the one mantra I tell myself every day is my own:

> *"Every day, in every way, we have*
> *the potential for change"*

I believe that every new day gives us an opportunity to live our lives differently. And every new moment does provide us with the potential for change.

We can choose to live life by a set formula, or we can think outside the box and realise new opportunities exist all around us. And we have the capability of creating new opportunities that can stretch us and grow us, and take our lives to a new level.

How we react to the challenges we face is a choice.

Always choose wisely.

What are three pieces of advice you can share for anyone trying to grow their own business brand?

o   Know what you stand for—be it quality service, outstanding results, hugely satisfied clients . . . Then, be that. Be that from day one; be that always. Be unwavering in your standards. Always honour what you stand for and aim for the very best in all you do. As I say to my clients, it's a matter of working to the Be-Do-Have philosophy: if you 'be' the very thing you stand for, you will 'do' and behave in that manner, and then you will 'have' it.

o   Give more than expected. Thrill and delight people by going the extra mile. Not only will you have happy clients, you will feel truly great about the additional value you have added to the lives of others. A well-worn copy of the Og Mandino book *The Greatest Miracle in the World* sits on my bookshelf and it contains within its pages a reminder of a principle which I have endeavoured to live by: go another mile. "The only certain means of success is to render more and better service than is expected of you, no matter what your task may be." It has served me well.

o   Do what is authentic for you. Be yourself. Be genuine and faithful to your own cause and sense of purpose. To not live authentically is to live by someone else's model of the world, someone else's expectations. It is so important to be truly congruent with who you really are.

There are so many ways to grow your business. There will be so many opportunities that will present themselves to you on your professional journey. And so many people with whom you could possibly do business.

Know how to be selective and trust your intuition. Ask yourself: is this the best thing for me and my business? Is it the right fit? Is this congruent with who I am and where I want to take my business? Is this going to add value to my business and the clients I wish to service?

What is your view on personal and professional development?

One of my highest needs is for growth. My personal behavioural profile is one that seeks to inspire and be inspired, so I have a voracious appetite for learning new things and reaching my greater potential, usually in experiential and motivating environments.

Continuing to grow and develop myself and my business is absolutely essential to my sense of achievement and the gaining of wisdom.

Surrounding yourself with the right people and the right influences will challenge your thinking and expand your horizons.

It's vital to model the excellence you observe in others, share space with the people who inspire you, listen to their stories, and learn from their learnings. Modelling excellence in mindset and behaviour is a sure-fire way to success.

For me, it's about taking the opportunities to gain exposure to the highest level of expertise in my fields of interest. This can be through any number of avenues, such as conferences, events, seminars, trainings, volunteering my services to gain new experiences, speaking engagements, webinars, on-line forums and groups, business memberships and affiliations, partnering, networking, reading, watching recorded events, listening to audio-recordings, and the list goes on. My advice is to do what works for you.

And, lucky me, my business is specifically about providing personal and professional development to my clients. As I am instrumental in my clients' growth journey, it is a given that I continue to build and refine my skills to serve my clients at a level of excellence.

Model the excellent thinking and behaviours of those who you most admire. You can't help but improve if you surround yourself with the right people.

What have been some of your most difficult challenges in business?

When you operate your own business, you have to be prepared to work both 'in' the business and 'on' the business; they go hand in hand. For me, my passion extends to both.

Adding value to the lives of others, enabling them to overcome what's keeping them stuck, helping them become empowered and realise their full potential, is what I do in my business.

Having a marketing and business development background, working on the business comes relatively easy to me. I enjoy creating and marketing, and taking my business to the next level.

But here's the thing; sometimes it becomes all-encompassing when you are passionate about everything you do. Enthusiasm and perfectionism can take over, and life can easily become all about business. Hardly seems a big issue if you love what you do right? However, we also know the importance of adequate sleep, healthy diet, quiet time for reflection, relaxation time to rejuvenate, fun time with family and friends, connecting with things beyond the self.

In operating my own business, managing my own work/life balance would have to be the greatest challenge.

To ensure I maximize my potential in all areas of my life, I have to put boundaries around work time, and my time outside of work.

It's important to notice when you are being all things in your business. At some point in your business's growth, you come to realise that you can't do it all. Enlisting the expertise of others who I can trust with my brand leverages my time and allows me to focus on core business, my clients, and have more control over work/life balance.

All the wins and challenges of business are opportunities for learning and growing. It keeps things interesting. Despite the challenges, I believe if you are passionate about what you do, have belief in yourself and the drive to succeed, then you will.

"Where focus goes, energy flows."

Tony Robbins

Have you ever felt like giving it all up to get a 'real' job?

I'm not sure that there is such a thing as a 'real' job—I think it's all about one's mindset and work ethic.

If by 'real' job one means steady 9-5 employment with a regular income, then sure, I've been there too, and I have been fortunate enough to work for some amazing, progressive organisations. There is so much to learn and so many opportunities to progress if you have the right work ethic and drive. One can still make profound differences and contributions from this platform.

Working as a solopreneur can have a little more challenge and uncertainty, but there is massive pay-off for those that thrive on variety and growth!

My personal work ethic has been the same whether I have run my own businesses or worked for someone else; whether in the private sector, government or not-for-profit; whether as a solopreneur or a team member; whether full-time or casual; whether a career-move role or a working-holiday role; whether I've been the boss or the worker-bee; it's all about giving the very best of yourself, in any given scenario, in order to bring about the best possible result in an ecological and value-adding way.

Being a solopreneur also brings freedom and choice — I choose who to work with, and when. I have the freedom to be flexible with my time; the freedom to do the things that I enjoy, and to be with the people I love. It enables me freedom of thought and of voice, where I live by my own values and rule-book and am driven by my own sense of purpose. I am able to align myself with like-minded people and to contribute to other people's lives, both professionally and personally.

> *"Choose a job you love, and you will never have to work a day in your life."*
>
> Confucius

Really being aligned with one's passion, and making a business or career out of it, that is the ultimate goal; and I'm so fortunate to experience this as The Change Agent. Of course, there will be some incidental things that must be done as part of running a business, though it's what's at the core of your business that matters—that's where the magic happens.

Every day I choose who I am as much as what I am. I evolve and grow with every encounter and with every client. I get to do what I love for my work.

Do what you love, and love what you do. That's what I call a 'real' job.

Gillian Skeer

www.creativecoach.co

Dr. Heidi Stieglitz Ham

Celebrating the unique abilities of people on the autism spectrum

"The person who tries to live alone will not succeed as a human being. His heart withers if it does not answer another heart. His mind shrinks away if he hears only the echoes of his own thoughts and finds no other inspiration."

-Pearl S. Buck

Dr. Heidi Stieglitz Ham has a passion for individuals on the autism spectrum and believes each and every individual deserves the best chance of finding their niche in life. Every person is unique and has something to contribute. Society doesn't always understand individuals on the autism spectrum or fully understand the pressure they face on a day-to-day basis as they try to fit in with mainstream society. Often, these individuals give their best but ultimately give up hope because they have exhausted all of their coping mechanisms and emotional resources. Many individuals become isolated and lonely as adults. Anxiety, depression, and attention deficit disorder (ADD) are a few of the challenges that individuals on the autism spectrum have to manage, but these symptoms are greatly reduced when an optimal environment is provided and others around them are accepting of who they are.

Dr. Heidi had a father with undiagnosed Asperger Syndrome. She also has a sister, four nephews, and a niece on the autism spectrum. She has seen firsthand the struggles that they faced and currently face, especially in their transition to adulthood. The difficulties arise for a variety of reasons; however, trying to fit into mainstream society, and failing time and again, was something that Heidi wanted to do something about. She could see that her sister and nephews were creative and intelligent but that they viewed the world from a different perspective.

Heidi has now started a community that celebrates the unique abilities of people on the autism spectrum. Individuals on the autism spectrum process information differently and their minds work differently to those without autism. These differences need to be celebrated and embraced. Heidi believes it is important to highlight the positive aspects of autism and share these remarkable gifts with the world.

The community is founded on three guiding principles. The first principle is to foster a community of people, both with and without autism, who lean on each other and provide support through the difficult transition from adolescence to adulthood and beyond. The next principle is to ascertain the interests, motivations, and desires of the individual on the spectrum to tap into what sorts of contributions they want to make to the world. This is where brainstorming and networking come into play. Putting individuals in touch with others who may be able to help develop their desires and providing practical and real-life experiences is one aspect of this process. Finally, a physical community will be developed where individuals can live through the transition to independence or choose to live in the community as a lifestyle choice.

Did you come from a family of entrepreneurs?

No, but I come from a hardworking family with a strong work ethic and a social conscience. My grandmother, Emma, was one of six siblings and they all grew up during the Great Depression in America during the 1930s. I was very close with my grandmother and her sister, Emily. Those two sisters, as different as they were, really shaped who I am today. I consider myself incredibly fortunate to have this invaluable experience.

My father had undiagnosed Asperger Syndrome. I wish that he had been diagnosed so he could have understood more about himself, and my mom, sister, and I could have understood him better as well. My father's memory for football statistics, facts, and numbers was amazing and he ended up working as a buyer for a steel company. He never missed a day of work, until he became ill, and he drove through the ice and snow about an hour each way, every day. At times, my father suffered from debilitating anxiety and he had a difficult time regulating his emotions. It was frightening, as a child, not understanding why his behaviour changed so drastically. He didn't understand his behaviour himself.

> *"Character cannot be developed in ease and quiet. Only through experience of trial and suffering can the soul be strengthened, ambition inspired, and success achieved."*
>
> Helen Keller

How did you come up with your business idea?

My nephew, 'J,' was diagnosed as a young child as having a speech and language delay as well as ADD but, sadly, the autism diagnosis was missed. Every year he seemed to slip through the cracks. He was discharged from speech and language therapy because the goals targeted the phonological processing disorder and he was not on any other type of therapy to help him with emotional regulation.

'J' was very interested in fireworks and science. After the American Independence Day celebrations one year, 'J' decided that he wanted to learn more about how fireworks were designed and how they exploded. He couldn't find any specific books in the library about how to design fireworks, but he did find one about making explosives. He checked out the book from the public library and proceeded to follow the instructions. After a few weeks, he was very proud that he made something that would explode and he shared this information with some of the kids at school. Unfortunately, this happened to be the year after 9/11 and the school alerted the authorities. Federal agents from the Bureau of Alcohol, Tobacco, Firearms and Explosives (ATF) raided my sister's home. 'J' and his family were not only traumatised but he was labeled as a 'bad' kid and, from then on, the school phoned the police for every incident.

'J' struggled in school and had a difficult time coping with social interactions, although he really desired to have relationships and friendships. During his school years, he was extremely anxious and just wanted to be part of a group. He ended up self-medicating with alcohol and drugs and wound up in further trouble with the law. 'J' is a very sensitive person and all he wants is a chance to work in an environment where he will feel accepted. He has tried to hold down various jobs over the years but they have not worked out for one reason or another.

Now, 'J' is a young man in his mid-20s. He has tried to live on his own, away from home, but he is unable to live independently at this time. 'J' needs a community of people to lean on. He has a strong desire to work and to contribute but he doesn't know exactly what he wants to do or what he can do at this time. This is where the networking strategies within the greater community can help. 'J' is very interested in sustainable living and his desire is to live somewhere where he can design a sustainable home, such as container homes. He wants to design systems that use alternative sources of energy. 'J' is a forward thinker and mechanically inclined and wants to become involved in sustainable living and organic farming. A sustainable living community would be the perfect option, not only for 'J' but for many other families searching for answers. Networking strategies are also important for others who are looking for ways to gain employment or contribute to the community. It is also important that the community includes a hub that fosters research and development.

> *"People, even more than things, have to be restored, renewed, revived, reclaimed, and redeemed; never throw out anyone."*
>
> Audrey Hepburn

What drives you on a day-to-day basis?

That is an easy question. The incredible need—families are desperate. I receive messages of support from families from the US and Australia who really need some new solutions for their loved ones on the autism spectrum. The ages range from teenagers through to mature adults. Here is an email that I received the other day:

"I've been searching for somewhere to reach out; my husband is fifty-four and just got diagnosed and is waiting to take the spectrum test. Thanks, I really love your autism community idea, I'll go to your sites, we are very isolated in this journey, his family is in denial, so I've been advocating for him alone. Thanks for all you do, I want to participate, help, somehow, we are willing to move anywhere."

Another email from a mother of a young man with autism:

"I love that the community you are working on will have something that promotes the value of people on the spectrum. To me, that is the most important message that needs to be spread loud and clear from the mountaintops. Aspies already do so much to try and fit in. There is only so much they can do and it's not fair (and I scream those words—not fair!!!) that they (or anyone) should have to change who they are to find a place in this world. People MUST learn to recognize and accept that others are different but that it is not something to fear or shun! Everyone has value. I long for a world that promotes that view. Thanks to you, the word is getting out."

When you think about community, it is about the people. Once we have a place where individuals on the autism spectrum feel understood and accepted and feel like they belong—that is the beginning of community. These individuals will have others (with and without autism) to lean on and they won't feel so alone. The other day, one adult man with

AS told me, 'Nobody understands what it is like to be completely alone.' He hasn't socialised in years and has been bullied his entire life. He is the kindest man you will ever meet and he doesn't deserve to be cast aside by society.

> *"You can design and create, and build the most wonderful place in the world. But it takes people to make the dream a reality."*
>
> Walt Disney

How do you stay inspired and motivated?

October of 2014 I was provided the opportunity to speak at TEDxPerth. A few weeks after the TEDxPerth talk was uploaded on YouTube, I received a call from a man who had watched the talk online. He was a mature man who had recently been diagnosed with autism. He wanted to see me and I asked him to come to my office. He arrived a few days later carrying several bags, one that held a wedding portrait of his mother, and his teddy bear. He carefully lifted the items out of the bag and placed them on the sofa next to him while we talked. I couldn't believe how vulnerable and sensitive this kind man was. He proceeded to tell me that he had been bullied much of his life but that at times he held down jobs and was a business owner prior to the global financial crisis.

This man continued to thank me and told me that nobody had been kind to him in many years. This broke my heart. Currently, his marriage is failing and he is looking for a place to live. I invited him to a small group evening with a few other adults on the autism spectrum, and he came and again brought his bags with the portrait of his mother. A few days later, he told me that it was the first time that he had been around people who accepted him for who he was since his mother died. This man is lonely but there are many other adults across the age groups who are lonely. Studies have been published reporting the dangers of loneliness.

At the end of the evening, he brought out his harmonica and played for the group. He told the group that he was once a drummer and when he was younger, he played in bands and knew a lot of well-known artists including the members of the DiVinyls.

This man needs a community. People to accept him and a place where he can play his drums and share his musical talent. He also still has years left that he could work doing something that is worthwhile to him. He told me that he really wanted to help other people.

> *"Loneliness and the feeling of being unwanted is the most terrible poverty."*
>
> Mother Teresa

When did you know your story could be a brand?

While I was researching and preparing for my TEDxPerth talk, I spoke with a property developer, who told me that I could develop one community, then make it successful, and then replicate it.

I realised that this story had a unique business proposition. One that would appeal to people that had a heart for adults with ASD as well as those who saw value in sustainable communities. Perhaps this idea has been attempted elsewhere but in Australia no one else has attempted this.

> *"The person who tries to live alone will not succeed as a human being. His heart withers if it does not answer another heart. His mind shrinks away if he hears only the echoes of his own thoughts and finds no other inspiration."*
>
> Pearl S. Buck

How critical is it to have a team to support you?

When one is crafting a vision, it is necessary to broaden the realm of ideas and this is best done with a combination of team members from diverse backgrounds. Their way of thinking and processing concepts can be a way to arrive at a solution that was completely unexpected. Certain individuals will possess skills that they can employ easily and in a way that motivates them to perform. These same skills may be pure drudgery to others. It is the integration of these varied abilities, personalities, and capabilities that can lead to accomplishing the ultimate goal. As long as all are united in a common approach with clear and conscientious leadership, the team will be able to succeed.

> *"Teamwork makes the dream work, but a vision becomes a nightmare when the leader has a big dream and a bad team."*
>
> John C. Maxwell

What have been some of your most difficult challenges in business?

I think the most difficult challenge has been to communicate to others my overall vision and then try to bring everybody on board in a unified fashion. Most people are interested in collaborating, but may want to start out very conservatively whilst others see the vision in its entirety and become very motivated to move ahead quickly to obtain funding to buy land and develop property.

Learning about the various funding options and business structures is not my strength but I understand that this is necessary for the idea to flourish and exist. Overall, if there is no business plan, marketing, funding and an organisation, this idea will be just that.

Have you always wanted to own your own business?

Yes, this is always something that interested me but I knew that I wouldn't take this leap until I had a business plan that would include individuals on the autism spectrum. I always felt strongly that there were not systems in place that could help these adults. I could see that they were graduating from high school and then nothing would happen, they would stay in their rooms in their homes not knowing where to even begin.

The idea of starting a community began in 2007 when I lived in Lagos, Nigeria. In Nigeria, many families live in rural areas and they do not have access to assessments or therapy. I started networking with an organization called Heart Spring in the US, who partners with organisations in third world countries. They shared with me a model that they called the China Model based on the work of Stars and Rain in Bejing. Families come to Stars and Rain for diagnostic assessment and parent training and then they go back to their villages and train their village how to perform the therapies.

I became ill in Nigeria and had to go back to the US and never received medical clearance to return to Lagos when my husband was working there. However, the dream never died and I still think of ways that I can help those individuals today. Working together with my sister, we started to investigate various types of solutions that might help "J" and I shared with her the model that I learned about through Heart Spring. My sister, who has Asperger Syndrome, is an organic farmer and also very knowledgeable about sustainability. She began sharing information regarding sustainable communities, but they were not suited for individuals on the autism spectrum because they had strict guidelines of who they would allow to live there. We decided in 2012 that a sustainable community would be the way forward. This would also open itself up to different types of investors. These investors may not have been drawn to a project about autism but drawn to the idea of sustainable living and alternative sources of energy. Other investors will be interested in autism and helping individuals find ways to contribute to society that work for them. This community will be very collaborative and bring together a wonderful team of great minds to provide hope to individuals on the autism spectrum and their families.

*"Continuous effort — not strength
or intelligence — is the key to
unlocking our potential."*

Winston Churchill

Dr. Heidi Stieglitz Ham

www.autismperth.com.au

Jane and Michael Pelusey

On a global trek to success

"The biggest adventure you can take is to live the life of your dreams."

Oprah Winfrey

A passion for travel, photography, and writing drew Michael and Jane Pelusey to create their own business, Pelusey Photography, in 2000. Michael was a professional photographer and Jane left her seventeen-year career as an ICU and trauma nurse. It was a brave and exciting step.

With more cheek than experience, they began writing articles for travel magazines and going on familiarity trips with tourism operators in the outback of Australia. They wrote for magazines such as *Australian Geographic, RM Williams Outback, Australian Country Style, 4WD Monthly*, and *Caravan and Motorhome Magazine.*

An article in children's magazine *Comet*, led to a connection to the publisher of the Primary Library section of Macmillan Education Australia. She recognised their emerging brand of outback travelers and commissioned the first six books *Living in the Outback*. This partnership alone led to seventy-five books in total.

Refining their mapping skills while researching 4WD tracks and camping locations led Michael and Jane to another book deal, this time with Hema Maps, and includes their best-selling *Western Australia 4WD Top 50 Trails Atlas & Guide.*

Their adventures would continue, and they'd walk the 1000km Bibbulmun Track, a highlight in Michael and Jane's life that also turned into a business opportunity developing a calendar and becoming trail assessors for the www.trailswa.com.au project.

Their experience of living a travel lifestyle where they adhere to the values of adventure, health, and fitness, gave Michael and Jane the idea to research the concept of the travel mindset: a way to live life to the fullest every day, both abroad and at home.

When did you know your story could be a brand?

It came about probably by accident, pointed out by other people! We had been running our business for about twelve months, writing for 4WD magazines and *RM Williams Outback* magazine. Our travel articles were outback-based, such as familiarity trips kayaking Ningaloo Reef and cycling in outback Western Australia and Northern Territory.

Because of our knowledge and love of the outback, a publisher asked if we would like to do a series of children's books about living in the outback. That led to a six-month journey around Australia, meeting and living with outback families. That book series of six led to seventy-five other books.

People would often introduce us as adventurers or travellers. Over time, we grew to own it and ran with that adventurer traveller brand.

We don't believe you can create a false brand just to sell something. If you are not coming from an authentic place, it won't ring true. Brand is about authenticity, truth, and trust.

How do you juggle your work/life balance?

We are lucky that our business involves something that we love doing and that we do it as a couple. For us, there is a very fine blurred line between work and life outside work. Many people ask if we ever have a holiday when we are not working. This question is based on the idea of not enjoying your work and therefore, needing to escape it. It reminds me of a quote from Seth Godin:

"Instead of wondering when your next vacation is, maybe you should set up a life you don't need to escape from."

One of our mindsets is to redefine what we call work and what we call life. As travel writers and photographers, work involves travelling. When we are on a familiarity trip enjoying a tour run by Navajo people in Monument Valley, we don't call it work. It is a life experience. When we are going out to dinner with the tourism representative in Vancouver, Canada, we treat it as meeting up with friends for a meal.

A friend of ours says, "There isn't a work/life balance—it is all life."

As a photographer, both for work and as a hobby, Michael can't or would even want to turn his photographic eye off. It is an artistic talent that goes everywhere with him. Similarly, ideas for books and articles come when you are out living life, not while sitting in the office working.

Our brand as adventurers, travellers and outdoor people is something we get to live twenty-four hours a day, seven days a week. A brand isn't something you can turn off and on. To be authentic, you need to be living it.

Do you think it is important to have hobbies or interests outside of business?

When I had a government job with high stress levels, I did believe you needed to have a life with hobbies unrelated to work: time to disengage, disconnect, and de-stress. This is dependent on not liking your job. In my days off and holidays, we would travel, go bushwalking, take photos, and explore. Then the opportunity to leave my old job appeared and we made the decision to create our business and lifestyle. Our business is traveling, bushwalking, and exploring, so in essence we have monetised our hobbies.

With all that being said, if our business was all-encompassing and restricted us from doing those things we love to do, that wouldn't work for us either. We also like to set time aside where we don't talk and do business just because we love it or we may miss out on other great opportunities and adventures.

What is your view on personal and professional development?

Personal and professional development is essential for anyone running his or her own business. As T. Harv Eker says, "your income can grow only to the extent that you do." The issue that can occur for business owners is getting caught up in the daily routine of running the business. There are times when you need to step away, learn some new skills, and learn about yourself. If your business is going to stay relevant and therefore profitable in this rapidly changing world, you need to keep on learning.

We have done professional development to improve our presentation skills, our writing and photography skills, our 4WD and survival skills. We have done personal development to learn about communication, interpersonal skills, and above all, ourselves. It's a continuous and ongoing part of our lives.

If you can walk away from a professional or personal development course feeling fabulous, inspired, and motivated it was worth the experience. However, my biggest tip is to document at least one big thing during the course that you are going to implement when you get back to work. It is so easy to arrive back and be sucked into the vortex of your business and lose track of what you learned.

What does a typical day look like to you?

Our typical day isn't particularly typical. We don't really have a routine for work. We do try and create our ideal day, every day, because we are in business to create a lifestyle, not just to be employed by our own business.

We usually start our day around 5am. This involves creating the best us physically, mentally, nutritionally, and spiritually. We start with a cup of tea in bed and some personal development reading. We may also watch a TED talk or an inspiring video.

Then we hit the beach for a run and a swim. There is nothing like getting the blood flowing to the brain for creativity and positivity. We may or may not stop for a coffee at a café. We do this for networking as well as mindset and enjoyment.

After our high-nutrition breakfast, we hit the computers. That may be working with our team, connecting with potential prospects, writing articles, blogs, or books, connecting with people on social media. On most days we meet up with clients or prospective clients for face-to-face time.

That is how the day usually pans out. That changes completely if we are traveling. We try to maintain the morning routine but the next hours could be anything, anywhere. We work wherever we are. We are mobile and flexible.

Did you ever feel like giving it all up to get a "real" job?

Jane left her real job in 2000. The hardest thing to get used to is the nature of the income. Our income comes in lump sums before and after projects and not in a fortnightly wage. So at times it can seem simpler to chuck it in and get a "real" job again. It isn't long, though, before we realize that the reality of a 9-5 is working for someone else, no flexibility, restrictions, and limited holidays. That realization is all it takes to get us into action.

What are you most proud of in your business?

We have achieved personal goals and at the same time left a legacy of education and knowledge. We've gotten to explore the world and ignited the curiosity in others, encouraging them to get out there and explore as well. When we first went into this business, we had no idea how to write a book. We trusted that the right people would show up at the right time to show us how.

We have turned our business into a lifestyle of our own making. That is of upmost importance to us. We can all work like dogs to make money, but if we have no time to do the things we want to do, there doesn't seem much point.

What inspired you to go into business?

Michael was already a freelance photographer. Jane's inspiration to go into business was desperation to live a life of freedom, unencumbered by shift work and limited holidays. In fact, it was a case of *you are not going without me*. Jane had the buffer of long service leave at half pay but she had no intention of going back.

We were really ignorant of what was going to happen and in some ways very trusting that it will all work out in the end. I heard this quote in the *Best Exotic Marigold Hotel*, but the original is:

> *"Everything is always all right in the end. If it isn't all right, then it isn't the end"*
>
> Ashwin Sanghi

What are three pieces of advice you can share for anyone trying to grow their own business brand?

Be authentic. Your brand will not ring true unless it is real and is something you are passionate about. Potential customers will be able to feel it. Simon Sinek says, "People don't buy what you do, they buy why you do it."

Know your values. We took some time to work out our personal and business values. You have to analyse your values away from the daily grind, so change locations, sit by the beach, or find a funky café. When you know your values and they are aligned with your brand, you can make decisions by reflecting on them.

You are your brand: Even though there is a separation between you and your business, you still are your business. How you show up can appear anywhere, on social media in particular. If your highest value is health and fitness, photos of you partying hard at an event may not be congruent with your brand. Whatever your product is, you need to be the product of that product.

What defines success?

Initially, we defined success as financial reward for the work that you are doing. That is what society expects and it is a very important part of the process.

However, if you are working 100 hours a week to make that amazing amount of money but do not have time to enjoy it with friends and family, it seems to be defeating the purpose of success.

Success is achieving our goals while being congruent with our values. Success doesn't have to conform to the societal norm. For us, it is our business providing us with a travel lifestyle, freedom, and flexibility.

But success is a very individual thing, so decide what it means for you. Our definition of success is not going to the same as everyone else's.

Jane and Michael Pelusey

www.pelusey.com

Josh Richards

On a mission to Mars

"Never let anyone define what you are capable of by using parameters that don't apply to you."

-Chuck Close

On a mission to Mars . . .

Physicist, explosives engineer, soldier, stand-up comedian and astronaut candidate—one thing Josh Richards can never be accused of is being boring.

In the last decade he's picked up booby traps for the Australian Army, slogged through mud with the British Commandos, used napalm in a music video for U2, been a science advisor to the richest contemporary artist in the world, and performed with some of the world's top comedians while wearing a giant koala suit to confused audiences from Los Angeles to Edinburgh.

Growing up, Josh had always loved all things science. It took a lifetime of unusual experiences for Josh to realise his dreams and find his purpose.

Josh found his true calling in late 2012 when he discovered the Mars One project. Selected from over 200,000 initial applicants, Josh is now one of 100 worldwide astronaut candidates short-listed to leave Earth forever and become the first to colonise Mars in 2025.

An in-demand professional speaker, Josh's storytelling makes for compelling and entertaining corporate keynote presentations that are *certain* to leave an audience with plenty to think about.

As an astronaut candidate with a natural talent for explaining complicated science, his public events and school programs inspire people of all ages to engage with science, and in doing so, discover the sky is **not** the limit.

If you had to do it all again, would you do anything differently?

Everything I have done has got me to where I am today.

I graduated from university with a degree in applied physics with no real clue how I would use it. I'd served with the Army as a Combat Engineer while studying, and had planned to transfer into bomb disposal, but my unit never processed the application.

Working with explosives in mining and construction was the next plan. I felt pretty useless though; like I had no real purpose. I was saving all this money and had no idea what to do with it. When a relationship crumbled, I left Perth to go to Melbourne where I planned to start a scuba diving business. Great fun learning all about the business, and was running the diving with sharks experience at the Melbourne Aquarium. But I was still lost. I'd applied to transfer back into the military, joining the Navy as a Clearance diver. But after going through boot camp a second time, the Navy told me the clearance diving school would be closed for 2 years.

So what was a young man meant to do with his life at this stage? Join the British Navy and became a Royal Marine (British Commando) instead! I endured the toughest and longest infantry training in the world and excelled. I had purpose and a career I loved. Just when things couldn't get any better, I was bitten by a deer tick and ended up with Lyme Disease and nearly died. I was twenty-four years old, a British Commando, and I couldn't even manage to walk up a flight of stairs. Although my recovery was nothing short of a miracle, after a lot of soul searching about my future, I realised I really didn't want to shoot people for a living. Once again with no ties and looking for purpose, I set off back to the UK to join Damien Hirst and the richest pyrotechnic sets in the world. It was awesome. Although it was a 9-5 job I was having a blast (excuse the pun), and I was also having fun on the side with stand-up comedy, speaking in schools and dabbling in many other areas. I even applied to work in Antarctica; I was still a little thirsty for adventure and a purpose to contribute somehow to mankind

What does a stand-up comedian and physicist do next? He applies to go to Mars, of course.

So to answer that question—No I wouldn't change a thing.

How important is family and friends to you on this journey?

As one of the last Mars Astronaut candidates, this question comes up a lot, as going to Mars is a solo journey from my family and friends.

Support is important to me, however, I have also learned that survival and independence is liberating. From being terrified backpacking and sleeping on the street after hotel mix-ups to completing the harshest military training, I know I can survive and thrive.

> "I feel like my purpose is to make a bigger impact on the world so I can serve many."

One of my fondest memories of being alone is living in the UK, meeting strangers every day.

As much as I love my family and friends, I feel like my purpose is to

> *"If your behaviour is modified from your 'failures' then they are not failures at all."*

make a bigger impact on the world so I can serve many.

What type of education do you value?

That's an easy one. I value an education that is diverse, interdisciplinary, and practical.

One that enables you to obtain broad knowledge, desire, and curiosity about all things.

I urge you to listen to lots of people, people from all walks of life, and of all ages, people you may not think have any value to offer. Listen to people who challenge you. These are the people you'll learn the most from.

There is no one size fits all. Everyone's journey will be different. What's important is to keep learning along your journey to finding your purpose. Then a whole lot more learning will be had.

Is failure a part of learning in a business?

Look at my past—Crash, burn, re-assess.

Minor failings with no learning could be completely useless. If your behaviour is modified from your "failures" then they are not failures at all.

I believe it's about recognising patterns of behaviours that lead to continuous failures.

You need to have amazing resilience to keep bouncing back.

If you had to choose another career, what do you think you would do?

Hmm. Current career—Astronaut candidate going to Mars.

That's pretty hard to top. If I had to choose though, at this stage of my life, it would have to be a spacecraft engineer or furthering my career in comedy and science communication.

I have always loved science and I love to share science with others, hence why I speak in schools to inspire kids to follow their science dreams. Who says you can't be an astronaut?

And it's not about me. If I can't get there, I can still be on a journey to help others get there.

Although I do love comedy, comedy as a career is a tough gig. I admire those who stick at it, because if often feels like training for a Mars mission or building spaceships is easier than stand-up!

What do you think you will be doing 5 years from now?

I will either be training to be an astronaut and my typical day may look like:

Building a space toilet, exploring geology, building and operating communication systems, and growing plants in greenhouses. Learning all the skills to be able to survive on Mars.

Or I may be in LA or Seattle, building spacecraft and sharing all things space.

Whatever happens with the Mars One project, I now know that I have a drive to explore.

Earth is not huge. I truly believe that it is critical for our species survival to explore and colonise other planets.

In five years' time I know that somehow, somewhere, I will be contributing to that adventure.

It doesn't matter where you are now or in five years. It always gets better if you want to give and serve others.

Describe some of the highlights of your business and career.

In my own business, some of the highlights have been:

Performing my debut solo show "Apocalypse Meow" to a full house at the 2011 Edinburgh Fringe Festival.

Standing up in front of a huge group of school kids and realising that my words were inspiring them to explore science and the possibilities that science can offer. They really cared about everything I had to say.

Completing a space science course with the International Space University.

Sitting in Starbucks in Brighton discovering an organisation that wanted to send people to Mars.

> "*If you don't explore you will never know what's out there.*"

Opening that email that stated "You have been selected from over 200,000 Mars One applicants worldwide to be in the final 100." Really, what can ever top that? Other than actually landing on Mars that is.

Is there anything else you would like to share about your journey that could help inspire others to follow their business dreams?

Whether they are personal, career, or business dreams, if you don't have goals you have nothing to dream about and nothing to work towards . . .

I don't really have the same strategy for setting your goals as others. Mine hasn't really been anything structured. I just knew I had dreams and I didn't want to be stuck in a job that I would end up hating. There was so much more to living than that. I knew I wanted to have purpose and I needed to go off and explore to know what those dreams would ever look like.

We sometimes set big goals just for the sake of it, without really understanding our purpose. You then achieve your goals only to be disappointed.

If you don't explore you will never know what's out there.

Josh Richards

www.themightyginge.com

Karen Livey

Developing Brain Savvy Leaders

"No problem can be solved from the same level of consciousness that created it."

-Albert Einstein

Karen started her career as a secondary school psychologist and geography teacher in Cape Town. After a year, though, she decided to broaden both her experiences and horizons, and that's when the fun and excitement began. She worked in the finance industry, health and fitness field, and finally, the world of technology.

Some years later, she bid adieu to her home country and headed off to fly, motorbike, and train her way across Europe to the UK. Once in the UK, she took up lecturing at a college, enjoying the opportunity to share her knowledge and experience in business and foundation insight of technology.

After another move, Karen needed to find new work, so back to the business world she went. It was tough, but she gained heaps of experience and worked with many amazing people.

Falling pregnant led to a change in focus, and Karen moved to Aberdeen, Scotland and completed her MBA a year after the babe was born. This was an enormous challenge, but she enjoyed the ride. She re-entered the world of teaching—a passion that still burned brightly. She lectured in Business Management, addressing many of the disciplines needed to achieve sustainable success.

There was still one more move Karen needed to make before settling down, and that was to Perth, Australia. She knew from the start that she was going to embrace her love for sharing knowledge and experiences

> *"The 'why' is really important—why do you want to start a business?"*

with others, as well as a drive to run her own business. She set herself up as a solopreneur.

She loved being a solopreneur as she discovered the power of neuroscience and neuroplasticity, completing a qualification in Neuroscience of Leadership. She now passes on this life-changing knowledge through presentations, speaking engagements, international conferences, and specialised leadership coaching.

Karen is an International Speaker and Director of Leadership Keys an organisation that delivers Brain Savvy Leadership programmes.

What advice would you give to someone thinking about starting their own business?

The "why" is really important—why do you want to start a business? What drives you to do this? Going into business to just make money is not going to work, not in the long-term. I learned that a long time ago, when I started a business in Aberdeen that I never really enjoyed. It was all hard work.

That heartfelt drive means you can dig deep when you are looking for that energy, that motivation to do something you are not that keen on doing. I am well-acquainted with procrastination, and have found my push to do some tasks come from a need to share my passion.

Having a support system is so important—from your nearest and dearest to those who are part of your inner circle. I have created an inner circle of positive people who provide both formal and informal support. It is reciprocal, which is vital for all of us. Sharing with others means you can put things into perspective. Too much and too narrow thinking can create obstacles that are probably surmountable; you just need to look at it differently, and your support people can help you with that.

My biggest challenge is creating a life balance that meets the needs of everyone around me. Family is extremely important, but you still need boundaries, and your family need to honour these. This is particularly relevant if you are working from home. I can so easily just pop into the office and do some more work, but I also need to remember that sometimes not doing a certain task is far more important than not managing my relationships properly.

You need to be prepared to keep going. If you believe in what you are doing, you are probably on the right track, although you may need to adjust. It is a matter of tenacity—if you know you have it, hang in until everyone else realises you do!

> *"It is a matter of tenacity—if you know you have it, hang in until everyone else realises you do!"*

> "*Don't become blasé about your achievements, no matter how small.*"

How do you stay inspired and motivated?

You can't stay inspired and motivated if you don't believe in what you do and have no support system to sustain you when you begin to flag.

Pick the people you surround yourself with carefully. They should have positive energy and grasp your vision. They will come to your rescue when you are looking for answers. I am able to tap into different people at different times, depending on the situation. Having that positive energy is incredibly important. There are too many people out there who have a negative attitude; walk away from them. They do not add value to your life.

Embrace the small wins. Each one is a step closer. Don't become blasé about your achievements, no matter how small. I recommend a "happiness" jar. Every day, write down those things that have given you a lift during the day. It may sound like something insignificant, but from a brain science point of view, it is incredibly powerful. Recognising yourself and what you have done is just as important as recognising others for their efforts and achievements.

Be grateful. Each morning I think about what I am grateful for. It can be a number of small things, or some mega (in my eyes) achievement. Whatever it is, it sets the scene for the day—it brings on those energy vibes, a must for being inspired and motivated.

The big one is to have time out—"me time." This can be anything you want it to be. I like to go for a cycle and swim with the dogs. I am a beginner cyclist, but in these moments I am away from the tangible world of staying in touch. It is all about remembering who I am and what truly makes me happy. Coming back to the office is a pleasure—ready for real action; inspired and motivated.

What is your view on personal and professional development?

Being a person who is in the "learning" business, building your skills base on both a personal and professional level is important. I can't imagine a life without learning; I love it. It does not have to be directly related to my profession either. Learning in different places from different kinds of people can translate into new and exciting products/services you can provide.

Your personal and professional development is interconnected—you can't do one without the other. Building from either side will result

No problem can be solved from the same level of consciousness that created it.

Albert Einstein

in you having a new experience, a new way of thinking, and/or doing. It's got to be good!

You also remain relevant and current—see how your industry is progressing, the new trends, and direction changes. Plus, you can "shout" about it to your customers/clients, letting them know you don't let the grass grow under your feet. From a customer perspective, it is good for them to realise you embrace the new concepts and/or products and are happy to incorporate them if it makes sense to your product portfolio and their business needs.

A side benefit to all of this is meeting new people, finding out what they do, how they work—broadening your horizons and making new connections. Everyone wins when you do this.

> *Learning is a treasure that will*
> *follow its owner everywhere.*
>
> Chinese Proverb

How important is innovation in business?

Innovation is about staying relevant—whatever that means in your business. If you are not innovating, you are not staying relevant. A lot of it is about looking at what I have available, and thinking about how I can re-purpose it. You may think that in the speaking business nothing much has changed, but the biggest one is using technology better.

Some people do amazing things to get their message across and to help you remember.

There is also the need to stay topical. My area of neuroscience of leadership is, in itself, very new. People and businesses are just beginning to hear about it. There has been a lot of talk about brain exercise, and there is a desire to take that trend and use it to my advantage to innovate to create a product that makes sense to people and works for them.

I believe that if I am not open to new ideas, I will grow stale. But having new ideas is not enough. My new ideas have to be commercialised, because, without that all I have is an idea. Trying to commercialise this new idea can be really difficult as we are always working with constraints, including time, availability, and resources.

The balance must be about being ready to take on and hear about new concepts and possibilities. Simultaneously, I need to figure out how to turn that into a service I am able to deliver and realise a return on.

> *Innovation distinguishes between a leader and a follower.*
>
> Steve Jobs

How important is resilience for success?

If you are not resilient, there is not going to be any success. You will have disappeared down the plug hole long before you know it. Being resilient is a foundation stone to achievement.

There is also a lot of talk about resilience these days. I look at it from both a personal and business perspective and see that business resilience is about being innovative and realigning the business to suit the current circumstances.

With regard to personal resilience, I acknowledge that I am a key player for my business. I do recognise its older cousin, Emotional Intelligence, which is necessary if you are going to have resilience. However, we tend to focus on the resilience part of the equation and sometimes forget about the former.

Emotional Intelligence is about managing your emotions, and sometimes that takes greater effort. I have found it helps to identify the feeling I have, say it out loud, and try to work out why I have this feeling. Where does it come from? Why is it so strong? That way I am able to build a resilient framework and watch out for those same triggers in the future. If they occur, I recall how to manage the emotion and can deal with it a lot more easily.

I also see resilience being intertwined with so many important aspects when running one's own business. Firstly, there is that passion. Then there is my support system; without it I could struggle for days. And, oh so critical is "me" time—time to regenerate all of my systems and be ready to embrace the world and its challenges.

A great example of resilience is Thomas Edison who said:

> *"I haven't failed. I've just found 10,000 ways that won't work."*

What have been some of your most difficult challenges in business?

As a solopreneur, my biggest challenge is having to wear so many hats. Some of the hats are the wrong size, but I need to squish them on my head all the same. There are some things I really enjoy doing, some not so much, and others not at all. Finding help with all the areas of my business that I know are not my strengths is critical for my business growth. Letting go is often a tough one for solopreneurs, and I am no exception.

Many entrepreneurs suffer from "bright shiny object syndrome." This means you can get easily distracted with something else that sounds much more interesting and more fun to do. Losing focus on shiny objects that don't make sense to your end game can be very dangerous. There was a time I was also very distracted about what others were doing and whether I should be going in a different direction. I have found it valuable working with a business coach to help me stay on track, focus on what I want and work towards my goals.

Another challenge for solopreneurs is the feast or famine cycle. If I am out there getting the business, I am not earning money. When I start earning the money, I am not looking for more business. Working on the business is just as important as working in the business. Define your role in the business and get others on board to work on or in if you need to.

Using technology and social media are other big challenges for me personally. Being able to keep up with technologies that can help me drive and grow my business is very time consuming and challenging as a business owner. I used to think this was only a challenge for the solo operator but the more I work in larger organisations I see it at every level across every industry.

> *The greatest glory in living lies*
> *not in never falling, but in rising*
> *every time we fall.*
>
> Nelson Mandela

I love these two quotes below.

Either you run the day, or the day runs you.

Jim Rohn

Master your strengths, outsource your weaknesses.

Ryan Kahn

How important is positioning in the marketplace?

Critical! If you don't position yourself, your product or your service correctly, don't be surprised when you get few people buying from you. You have to know who you are selling to; that is, your target market. If your aim is wrong, your product will be wrong for them.

This applies whether you are looking from a local, regional, national, or even international level. Customers are highly sophisticated, with the Internet at their fingertips to check and compare your offerings with others.

Careful and clever branding will help your positioning. If there is a mismatch between your branding and delivery once again, say goodbye to sales and your position in the market place.

There are some adverts on the television that I think are awful, or ridiculous, or just unpleasant, but I have realised I am not their target audience—I just happen to be watching. They have profiled their 'shopper' and aim it directly at them.

Building my brand to match where I want to position my service in the marketplace is pivotal to my success.

Karen Livey

www.leadershipkeys.com.au

Luke Versace

The Law of Winning

"If winning isn't everything,
why do they keep score?"

-Vince Lombardi

In 2002, at the age of nineteen, Luke decided to travel around the world. One of his first stops was to Spain's famous Running of the Bulls. As a talented but unfocused sprinter, Luke assumed it'd be easy enough to stay out of the bulls' way. Just thirteen seconds into the running, though, Luke was gored, twice in the left leg, and suddenly found himself in need of emergency surgery if he did not want to lose his limb. Though surgery was successful, Luke found himself overcome with emotion and the desire to win the Stawell Gift, Australia's most prestigious professional footrace. Winning this would not just be a personal goal for him, but as a way to thank his parents for the support they had shown him over the years.

Success did not come right away, however, and it wasn't until 2014 that Luke was finally able to make his vision of winning the Stawell Gift a reality. He dedicated the win to his parents.

Whilst known for his athletic achievements, Luke has also enjoyed success an educator and lawyer. He combines these pursuits with public speaking, training, and consulting. Luke uses his personal and professional experiences to provide rare and valuable insights into what it takes to win no matter what the circumstances.

Speaking with honesty, humour, and, at times, irreverence, Luke has the rare ability to equip his clients with the knowledge, skills, and motivation to fulfil their potential and reach their goals.

Luke achieves this by sharing 'The Law of Winning,' a combination of innovative and time-tested principles, proven to be vital to succeeding in competitive environments. Using these principles, Luke helps his clients to critically assess their performance and identify both organisational and individual strengths, as well as areas of untapped potential.

But it is Luke's ability to help his clients understand why they excel in some areas and not others that his true value as a speaker and trainer can be seen. Helping his clients to better understand themselves and the environment they operate in allows Luke to assist in the development of innovative yet practical strategies that can immediately improve performance.

A raging bull couldn't stop Luke from achieving his goals, so unless you have you have a herd of them in your way, the chances are, Luke can help you achieve yours.

How do you stay motivated and inspired?

Finding the motivation to continue pursuing a goal even when things aren't going to plan is one of the most difficult challenges that anyone can face and unfortunately is a common part of establishing and running your own business.

> *"The secret to maintaining my motivation and inspiration when times are tough is to understand why I am trying to reach the goal or goals that I am."*

The secret to maintaining my motivation and inspiration when times are tough is to understand why I am trying to reach the goal or goals that I am.

I first discovered this approach during my athletics career, when I realised that in spite of the setbacks—such as being gored by a bull or losing form and confidence—I never lost the desire to continue pushing on. I was motivated to win the Stawell Gift to reward my parents for the love and support they gave me through my darkest days.

In terms of my speaking and training business, I am driven to push through any challenges that may present themselves because I love helping people fulfil their potential and reach their goals. In addition to seeing my clients succeed, I also am driven by a desire to be able to establish a financially sound business that I can primarily run from home. I want to be able to spend as much time as possible with my family, whilst at the same time being able to earn enough money so that my wife and I can give my son every opportunity to live his dreams, whatever they may be.

When did you know your story could be a brand?

In the weeks and months following my victory in the Stawell Gift, it became apparent that my story of overcoming adversity resonated with people from a diverse range of backgrounds.

In particular I found that people could easily relate to my struggle to reach my potential and achieve my goal of winning the Stawell Gift. People were interested in how these struggles and the frustration they caused ultimately shaped me as an individual and gave me the insights into what it takes to succeed—insights that I today share with my clients.

It wasn't until I began speaking to corporate audiences, however, that I realised my professional experiences as a lawyer and educator, as well as those I had as an athlete, had the potential to be combined and transformed into a brand.

What is your view on personal and professional development?

Personal and professional development is essential to succeeding in life and business. The satisfaction that accompanies such growth and development is a great feeling and one that I find extremely rewarding.

I am the first to admit, though, that such development is not always easy to achieve, in large part because before such growth can occur, a person must be willing to undertake an honest—and at times—critical assessment of not only their strengths, but also their weaknesses.

This is a challenging task and I know it was one I avoided throughout the early stages of both my professional and athletics career. As a result, I failed to identify the areas I needed to improve in and this resulted in me failing to fulfil my potential, which prevented me from achieving my goals.

> "*Personal and professional development is essential to succeeding in life and business.*"

Over time I realised that as painful as this process might be in the short-term, failing to reach my goals was far worse. Now, I regularly take the time to self-assess so as to ensure I am giving myself the best chance I can to achieve my goals.

> *"One of the most significant lessons I learned during my athletics career was to regularly set goals."*

I teach many of my clients about this process so that they too can ensure they are developing themselves as quickly and efficiently as possible.

Do you set regular goals?

One of the most significant lessons I learned during my athletics career was to regularly set goals. Initially this was as simple as saying 'I want to win the Stawell Gift.' As time went on, I realised that whilst having a long-term goal was great, I needed a number of short-term goals, which, if achieved, would bring me closer to achieving my long-term goal.

This approach also helped maintain my motivation, as I was able to enjoy the satisfaction that accompanies achieving a goal more regularly. These mini victories also helped build my confidence.

I continue to utilise this approach as I build my speaking and training business. My end goal is to have a sustainable and financially viable business; for this to happen I must firstly achieve a number of smaller, short-term goals. These include developing my products and services so they provide maximum value for my clients, continually taking or creating opportunities to grow my brand, and further refining my speaking skills.

Do you think it is important to have a mentor?

Having a mentor or mentors continues to play an important role in the attainment of my goals. There is a great deal that I have to learn, not just about business but also life, and as such I proactively seek the guidance and advice of people who can help teach me the lessons I need to learn in order to succeed.

> "Failure can play a role in teaching you what you need to know in order to succeed.

Over the course of my life this role has been performed by a range of extremely talented and selfless people, beginning with my parents who taught me the importance of hard work and persistence. Then there have been teachers, athletics coaches, and even friends who have at one time or another acted as a mentor to me.

Today I continue to utilise a variety of mentors, each who are helping to ensure that I give myself the greatest chance of reaching the goals I have set. Together, these individuals have had a profound impact on me. Without their assistance, I simply would not be where I am today.

Is failure a part of learning in business?

Failure is most certainly a part of business, just as it is a part of life. Whilst failure and the disappointment that accompanies it is never an enjoyable feeling, it can play a role in teaching you what you need to know in order to succeed.

This is a message that I am constantly sharing with all of my clients and is one that I learned throughout the course of my athletics career, where for almost a decade I fell well short of reaching my goals. The key is to understand why you failed. This can be difficult, as many people often feel so dejected or even embarrassed by their failures that they try and just forget about them and move on with their lives as quickly as possible.

However, if you are willing to confront failure head on, understand why it happened, and then learn from it, you can drastically reduce the chances of that failure occurring again.

I apply this philosophy to my business regularly. If a keynote address doesn't run as smoothly as I would like, I ask *why*? Then make changes. If my marketing materials aren't getting the response I want I, I ask *why*? Then make changes.

I don't know everything and will make mistakes. The key is to learn from those mistakes and to do my best not to make them again.

What type of education do you value?

I value any educational experience that develops me as a person and equips me with skills and knowledge I can later use to help achieve my goals.

Whilst I have certainly enjoyed this benefit from the formal education I received studying law, commerce, and teaching at a tertiary level, I believe it was lessons I have learned out of the classroom which have taught me the most. It is these I value above other types of education.

> "*The key is to understand why you failed.*"

I say that because these 'life lessons' taught me the most about myself. They taught me about my strengths and weaknesses and helped bring into focus what was important. As a result I was able to set myself goals that, although challenging, were within my reach if I performed at or near my best.

Interestingly, the times where I made decisions regarding the goals I wanted to achieve coincided with moments in my life where I was at my lowest. The most noteworthy example of this was when I set myself the goal of winning the Stawell Gift as I was being wheeled into surgery following being gored by a bull.

> "Today the greatest challenge I face is to continuing growing my business."

Today I continue to use these lessons and share them with my clients, all of whom have at one time or another found themselves in difficult situations in either a professional or personal capacity. What I tell them is that whilst such situations might seem like negative events, they can be used to sharpen their focus, clarify their goals, and be used as motivation — all of which are vitally important if they are to reach their full potential.

What have been some of your most difficult challenges in business?

Throughout each stage of developing my speaking and training business I have confronted challenges. In the infancy, it was trying to get a grasp on how my journey and the lessons it taught me could be turned into a brand.

This task was made difficult because not only did I know very little about the speaking and training industry, I also felt embarrassed about promoting myself publicly as someone who understood what it took to be successful. Although I knew I had an intimate understanding of this topic, the years of disappointment and failure I had endured prior to achieving my goal made it hard to accept that others saw me as a winner.

Ultimately I overcame this by incorporating my struggles into my brand story and this has actually enhanced my ability to get my message across. The people I work with find it easy to relate to someone who hasn't always found it easy to succeed.

Today the greatest challenge I face is to continuing growing my business. Whilst I have been able to achieve this largely through word of mouth referrals from satisfied clients, I know that if I am to reach my goal of having a sustainable and profitable business over the long-term, I will need to continue to develop and refine the way I market myself.

How important is it to have a distinctive brand?

Having a distinctive brand is vital to the ongoing success of my speaking and training business. In fact, together with delivering high-quality services that significantly improve the performance of my clients, my brand is the single most important factor in determining my success.

In order for my message to have the impact it needs to inspire the behavioural change in my clients, they must first believe that I know what I am talking about.

I take great care in ensuring that both my current and prospective clients not only know my story, but understand how it equipped me with the skills and knowledge to help them fulfil their potential and enjoy the success they crave.

When I reflect on my experiences as an athlete, I think about the times I was at my lowest and it looked as though my dream of winning the Stawell Gift had passed me by. I can clearly remember having countless conversations where people would tell me that I would never win the race and that my athletics career was over.

These people weren't trying to be negative or put me down—most were friends or people who were trying to help me and they were just giving me their honest opinion. Although I respected them for having the guts to tell me to my face, I can truly say that no matter how bad things got, I never stopped believing that I could turn things around.

Today I share this message with my clients, almost all of whom have dreams or ambitions that others think are beyond them and I tell them that as long as they believe they can do it, they will.

Luke Versace
www.lukeversace.com.au

Shannon Bush

Leading you to Creative Possibilities

*"A business has to be involving,
it has to be fun, and it has to
exercise your creative instincts."*

-Richard Branson

Spending time in and around business has been a part of Shannon's life for as long as she can remember. She didn't necessarily know what role she might take on in the business world but there was little doubt in her mind that being in business was going to be part of her future.

Her entrepreneurial spirit was ignited around the time she started school as she realised the things she loved to make could perhaps be things that she could also sell. This was the start of her fascination with aligning creativity and innovation with business.

Shannon absorbed everything around her, learning what it was like to interact with customers and how to deliver quality service. She listened to stories, participated in business discussions by asking a lot of questions, and began to realise that the world of business was indeed a place she felt at home in.

While she initially ventured into what would be called a 'traditional career' her natural curiosity and tenacity bought her back to her business roots and have been key to her success. She has always been interested in understanding people and helping them to better understand themselves. Her voracious appetite for learning means she has completed many courses and immersed herself in the world of business and personal development.

> *"One of the most powerful beliefs instilled in me was that it was possible, as a woman, to be a success in business."*

In 2009, Shannon founded Creative Possibility. It has become known as a place where business, leadership, and creativity unite to offer specialist coaching and workshop solutions to business owners and leaders committed to growing themselves and their organisations to a place of effortless success. It has become the vehicle for Shannon to express the things she loves the most: business, people development in the form of personal and business leadership, creativity, and innovation. Creative Possibility has offered her a chance to create a lifestyle that allows her to travel, continue to learn, spend time with incredible people and give back to the community.

What beliefs did you have growing up about business?

As a young child, I was blessed to spend a significant amount of time with family members who were leading small businesses. My grandparents on both sides of my family had been business owners and my dad also had small retail businesses. Little did I realise that the hours I spent during school holidays and at weekends in and around these businesses were laying the foundations for me to step into business myself in the future.

I learned valuable lessons about a whole raft of things from customer service through to pricing for profit through to definitions of success and the role of education in business. Though the beliefs instilled in me were diverse, I have had to challenge some of them both in my corporate career and now as an entrepreneur and small business owner.

One of the most powerful beliefs instilled in me was that it was possible, as a woman, to be a success in business. It was also possible to create business success by being original, creative, and different. These beliefs underline the core message I want to share with all I do at Creative Possibility; that when business, (personal) leadership, and creativity unite, success occurs and individuals and teams thrive.

> *"Education is the key to being able to change circumstances and to create new experiences and outcomes."*

What is your view on personal and professional development?

I have always loved learning and I strongly believe education is the key to being able to change circumstances and to create new experiences and outcomes. Learning fosters a curiosity and inquisitiveness to understand and evolve, which in turn supports innovation, creativity, and success.

We learn at every stage of our lives. Even if you don't recognise the learning, it's there and happening. Knowledge is a powerful asset that allows you to achieve what it is you want—a dream business, a dream life, or something else. It creates an awareness, and in turn, that awareness provides you with insight to support your growth in business and life. New knowledge and skills help you be innovative and think outside the box. When you actively commit to developing yourself personally and professionally you are putting yourself at a distinct advantage over others who have not made the same commitment.

Personal and professional development lead to skill enhancement and the development of theoretical expertise, which increases professional credibility and in many instances, assists you to create confidence and trust with your customers and clients. A mind open to active learning is an inquisitive, curious mind and one that is more readily open to new discoveries, new beliefs, and new opportunities. Don't ever be afraid to admit you have more to learn, and be proactive about getting out there and discovering what there is to learn.

How important is innovation in business?

Innovation is key to success in business. Continuing to do the same things you have always done creates significant stagnation. The reality is we live in a fast-paced, technologically-focused world where our clients and customers are being asked to process and evaluate information at an increasingly alarming rate.

What this has led to is substantial overwhelm for many consumers and businesses. Innovation is your opportunity as a business leader to genuinely stand out from the crowd and be noticed by your ideal market for the right reasons. While creativity is not innovation, the two are intricately related and work well hand in hand.

"I am not creative" and "I am not innovative" are common beliefs held by many business owners. The reality is something quite different. Being in business asks you to be creative every day. It asks you to innovate and to refine or even reinvent yourself and your products and services on a frequent basis.

The business landscape is ever-evolving and a new style of business leadership is being called forth. This new style leadership is founded on attributes including creativity and innovation. Right-brain leadership,

> *"I find that my goal-setting sessions provide me with a structure to dream bigger and bolder and to capture the vision that details where I am headed."*

as I call it, is the kind of leadership that will support business at every level so they survive well into the future.

Do you set regular goals?

I have been a goal setter for as long as I can remember and I love setting goals.

Over the years I have worked with clients as a business and executive coach and workshop leader, I have found it fascinating how many people don't set goals. I have heard hundreds of reasons why goal-setting doesn't work and why it is a waste of time.

I find that my goal-setting sessions provide me with a structure to dream bigger and bolder and to capture the vision that details where I am headed and the potential ways I might get to my personal version of success. In its simplest form, goal-setting is about mapping out what you want. It is your opportunity to capture, in words, or with images, what you've probably been dreaming about for years.

Goal-setting is the cornerstone of business planning. I lead dedicated workshops each year to teach people, by way of goal-setting, how to clarify what they want to achieve as a byproduct of their business or role.

Something I have noticed again and again is that those who don't set or follow goals and plans behave in this way for a variety of reasons.

Whatever those reasons are, though, I invite you to rethink goal-setting as a fun part of your business. It is your chance to capture the big bold dreams you have and to detail what you want to accomplish in life and the variety of exciting and creative ways you might just be able to do that.

How important is money mindset in business?

The right kind of mindset is critical in business and money mindset is just one vital factor that actively contributes to the kind of mindset that supports business and entrepreneurial success.

Shortly after starting Creative Possibility, I found my own mindset challenged by the reality of being in business. I realised that the money part of my mindset was playing a significant role in holding me back and limiting my wealth growth.

At the time I was fortunate enough to learn about a new coaching certification in money mindset and I instantly signed up. While much of the processing was confronting and challenging, it provided me with much personal growth, helped me to reframe my beliefs around money and my own sense of personal and professional worth, and has provided me with a rich toolbox to access to support my clients.

> "Growth is the underlying action sitting at the foundation of every successful business."

One of the most rewarding things I have coached clients through is uncovering and understanding the role of their money story. Stemming from childhood, your money story underpins most of the beliefs you develop related to money, worth, value, abundance, and wealth. If your money story is filled with experiences that taught you money was a bad thing and not something to be earned freely and used for good, then imagine what sort of impact that could have on your business results. It's this sort of money mindset that supports you to be poor, or to make money and lose it through mismanagement or unsound investment.

One of the most significant money mindset transformations I experienced was with a client who had held tightly to a belief that the only way to make money was through crime. Her family life growing up was filled with experiences that supported this belief and painted the picture that it was a truth. When it came to growing her service business and being paid well in exchange for her extensive expertise, she struggled with her feelings about the wealth growth of her business. On more than one occasion she said, "I feel like I am robbing people." She wasn't. The investment her clients were making was a fair exchange for the support and learning they received. Over time, and only after unraveling and challenging every part of her money story, was she able to create a set of new money beliefs and a new money mindset that supported her and her future.

Is growth an essential strategy for survival?

Yes!

However, it depends on what type of growth, as not all growth in business allows for survival to be achieved and for success to eventuate. Growth is the underlying action sitting at the foundation of every successful business, and if a business is successful then it is a business that has survived, and it is one that has thrived, the ultimate in survival.

When I first started out as a sole trader I realised, thanks to my natural planning and goal-oriented personality, that having a detailed plan, that mapped out what I wanted to achieve and by when, was the core way for me to measure and be aware of my progress in business. It was my tool to map out what I wanted and therefore it became my survival plan; my business growth plan.

I knew the plan needed to be exciting, motivating, and focused so that it mapped out the direction I wanted to travel in and how I would know when I had arrived at that destination. From this initial planning I created a framework I used for my own business and life and then, after accomplishing my goals and surviving and increasing my success, I began using the same method—something I call the Effortless Success Framework—with my clients with great success. This strategic survival tool supports business, wealth, expertise, and self-growth to guide a business owner or leader to grow in the right way.

What do you believe holds people back from achieving their dream business or life?

Themselves and their beliefs!

That might seem a simple answer and yet the reality is it is quite complex. I've had the privilege of working closely with business owners and employees from many diverse industries. With a background that includes a lot of people development and qualifications and experience as a therapist and counselor, I have had an insight into how, as individuals, we are motivated, what leads to the inner drive we can all access, and the things that get in the way of achieving our ultimate goals.

What I have observed most of all is a core belief of not being enough… The belief may not be influential all the time but it can and does show up at times when it's generally most unwanted.

It has many masks. Sometimes it shows up as "I'm not good enough" or it might appear as "I'm not clever" or "I don't know enough." I have seen it show up in people as "I'm not experienced enough," "I'm not young enough," "I'm not confident enough," and even "I'm not attractive enough." I am sure there are times you can remember when you've tried to understand something and "I'm not _____ enough" has been a part of your internal (or external) dialogue.

> "What do you believe holds people back from achieving their dream business or life?
>
> Themselves and their beliefs! "

What have been some of your most difficult challenges in business?

When I first started my own business one of the biggest difficulties was getting really clear on what it is that I was offering and the benefits for my clients.

Like many people leading a service-based business, I stepped into my business with a lot of valuable experience and with a wealth of knowledge and training, but I didn't really know what to do first or even how to be a business owner. Despite my exposure to small businesses and years working in business at a corporate level, facing small business ownership as a reality can be a pretty scary thing. Much of the time, small business owners have limited experience in business. The business landscape is ever-changing and confusion can reign as to where to invest your time, your commitment, your money, your emotions, and more.

I experienced this firsthand, but feel grateful that my creative and innovative nature and commitment helped me to quickly address many of the knowledge limitations so that I could move forward and progress relatively quickly on my path to success.

I feel lucky that I have continued to positively grow my business each year since I started. That is not to say there haven't been times when I have wanted to throw it all in and go back to a regular paying job. I made a commitment to myself that I'd give this business everything I have and that means staying focused, getting help in the form of training and coaching, creating balance that supports me and the people closest to me, saying "yes" to opportunities even when they scare you silly, and daring to celebrate every step of the way.

Obstacles will arise. How you respond and react to them and how quickly you can refocus and get back on track make all the difference to the impact they have and the end result you experience.

Shannon Bush

www.creativepossibility.com.au

Sharon Brown

**Creating health, harmony
and prosperity.
The Feng Shui way**

*"All the flowers of all the tomorrows
are in the seeds of today."*

-Chinese Proverb

Sharon

Brown was first introduced to Feng Shui in the mid 1990s, after reading what little was available on the subject back then. She has since become an educator and leader in the Feng Shui industry for the better part of fifteen years and has over twenty years of business experience. She trained under a number of Feng Shui teachers such as Grand Master Raymond Lo of Hong Kong.

Sharon is the Master of Global Palace of Feng Shui and Master Visioneer of Vision Boarding International. Well qualified in the area of Feng Shui, Sharon still continues to develop her skills and knowledge with some of the best teachers in the world.

Sharon loves sharing the many benefits of Feng Shui to clients, students and organisations from around the globe through her Feng Shui consultations and classes. She has trained many of the current Feng Shui practitioners in Australia; hence earning the respect and title of Master of Feng Shui by her students and graduates.

As an expert in Feng Shui, Sharon has appeared on many lifestyle television and radio programs She is well-published as a contributor to numerous magazines and is the author of *4 Pillars of Destiny—the Feng Shui Way*. Her next book *Picture Your Future* will be a must-have resource in the area of vision boarding and goal setting.

She is a wife of twenty-five years to Steve, a mother to an amazing daughter Shayla, and mother to the business mascot, Miss Fu.

Did you come from a family of entrepreneurs?

I have a great-grandmother who was a widow at a young age, with a precocious six-year-old daughter. Still, she set up two businesses in their small village in Scotland. She was a very gifted seamstress, and she hand-sewed beautiful gowns. She also set up a little confectionary shop in the front room of her home. It was unheard of for a young woman to operate her own business in the early 1920s, let alone be a single mother. I admire her tenacity greatly!

As a child, my dad would attend seminars; he was always inventing something and would be listening to motivational people. I have some old and treasured books by some of the greatest entrepreneurs of their day, such as Dale Carnegie, Og Mandino, Michael Le Bouf and W. Clement Stone. I remember my dad listening to *Acres of Diamonds* by Dr. Russell H Conwell on the old cassette player when I was about ten years old and the impact it had on me. My parents received a call from the school that same year as I had begun selling chocolate crackles to the other children for about .10c each. The principal informed my parents that I was in trouble, as this was not allowed; my dad told the principal that I should be praised instead of reprimanded.

My dad brought his daughters up to believe we could do anything we put our minds to. We were never, ever reprimanded if we came home with a bad grade in our school reports, however, if there was a comment that we didn't try our best or we had a bad attitude—that was entirely a different story.

My dad has been passionate about photography since he was sixteen-years-old, and in his early sixties, decided to attend university to get a degree in it. He was the oldest student in his class to graduate. He is now in his 70s and still studying away completing online courses. He is such an inspiration and we continuously bounce ideas off each other.

> "*Innovation is paramount for a business to evolve and grow*"

Do you think it is important to have a mentor?

They are a must and having an awesome coach
or mentor is critical to the success of any business; you can't afford not to have one! For quite some time I never even realised I had mentors. Mentors are the people who have travelled a similar path and are there to help and guide you through yours. In the early years of my business life, I wasn't in a financial position to afford a mentor or a coach (not all are paid either; sometimes mentors just take you under their wing). I then met someone who did basic business coaching and I began to see the value.

I have now had a few coaches and mentors throughout my business journey and have received something special from every one of them. An awesome coach won't just talk about facts, figures, marketing and sales, as important as these are. They will also hold you accountable when you say you're going to complete something. They will really get to know who you are and will respect your values and goals. .

How important is innovation in business?

Without innovation, your business will became stagnant; it may even dry up and become redundant and obsolete. Innovation is paramount for a business to evolve and grow; it creates excitement and anticipation. It also keeps our creative juices flowing and allows us the opportunity to experiment in new and exciting offerings.

Is failure part of learning in business?

Back in the mid 1990s I started a clinical aromatherapy and massage business in a medical centre. I made the mistake of going into it with another person who was a beautician; within six weeks she packed up her side of the business and left me with her outstanding debts to run it on my own. I had to make the tough decision to move the business to a home-based business as I just couldn't keep up with the expensive outgoings. I battled to keep it going for a couple of years before I was forced to close and go off to work in an office. It was a huge failure in my eyes back then and something I really took to heart, so I took it particularly hard.

Looking back, I now know it was doomed from the start as the correct structures, planning and offerings were never in place. I learned that no matter how great you are in your chosen field or industry, without having knowledge about marketing, sales, and understanding your financials, you are setting yourself up for failure.

Many years later, there have been many 'failures' in my journey; however, I no longer view them as 'failures;' I now view them as 'lessons.' And whenever one appears, I step back and see what it is I need to be learning from the experience and inevitably my business and life grows and evolves in a more positive way.

How important is resilience in business?

Many times in business we get knock backs, we can get criticised, judged and challenged. Without having resilience and mental strength, my business would not be as successful as it is today!

One of my favourite quotes and mantras is "That which doesn't kill you only makes you stronger." You look at any adversity that gets presented to you and you figure out a way of turning it into a positive. I used to worry all the time about what my competitors were doing, one day my dad said to me, "If you are so busy minding somebody else's business, who is minding yours?" Wise words indeed!

Is speaking part of your marketing strategy?

I first used speaking as part of my marketing strategy in 2001; I had gone from full-time employment to a job share in order for me to get my new Feng Shui business started. I decided to hold a Feng Shui Information Seminar in order to promote my Feng Shui consultations and gain more business. At school I was the kid in the corner who wanted to be invisible and I certainly was not a speaker. I figured if I had twenty people attend this seminar, I would be happy. I ended up with seventy people! As nervous as I was, once I got past the introduction—in a very shaky, dry voice—and started talking about my topic, I was in the zone and my information flowed. It was a massive success with over thirty new consultations booked. At the beginning of the following week I was able to resign from my job share employment.

I began doing more seminars, then building on to this presenting different modules. I was a guest speaker at different organisations and networking groups, was interviewed on the radio; I featured on a couple of lifestyle shows on television, and became a paid professional speaker to an international law firm in five cities around

> "There have been many 'failures' in my journey; however, I no longer view them as 'failures;' I now view them as 'lessons.'"

Australia. Speaking gave me credibility and confidence; it has also given me an incredible amount of new clients and students.

What do you believe holds people back from achieving their dream business or life?

Self-doubt in their abilities or that they can make their ideas into a viable business. They may not have any support from their family members. Support from family and friends I believe is crucial, even if they don't really understand everything about your business. I think it is more about having people around you who believe in you. In my Picture Your Future Seminars, I teach people about visualising their idea or dreams.

Isolation can also be quite debilitating in business, especially if they are a home-based business. They tend to hide behind the safety of their computers, mobile phones, and social media. I would encourage all business owners to attend relevant networking events, seminars, conventions, and business breakfasts/sundowners, or even join some business associations. CONNECTING face-to-face is exceptionally powerful and this has been one of the most successful ways of gaining new clients and being around like minded people, I attended a business association breakfast a couple of days ago; within five minutes of introducing myself to a women she asked if I would be interested in speaking to about one hundred and fifty people as a guest speaker! An opportunity to speak to 150 prospective clients, who wouldn't want that?

Continuous learning is critical to sustaining and building a business as is being open to changing what has always been done that way. Listen and learn, learn and listen some more and always be open to new ideas.

Sometimes, we get so busy working *in* our businesses, rather than *on* our business that we become overwhelmed and unable to grow our business. It is important to be able to step back from the business and breathe. My favourite thing is to take my little dog with me to walk along the beach and then sit on a rock to meditate, visualise, and converse with the Universe as to what I want to attract to my life. Not everything has to be about business either; it is so important to have a balance. Health, holidays, and family time will always take priority, as without these my world would be very hollow and empty!

What have been some of your most difficult challenges in business?

Feng Shui for some can appear a bit out there, a bit woo woo, so to have my business taken seriously was one of my major challenges. In the early years, whenever I would go to networking events, some people would ask if what I did was a real business, some would politely excuse themselves, and then there was the occasional person who would scoff or laugh and say it was a load of rubbish!

A few years ago I went through one of the toughest periods of my life. I sold my previous business, my marriage came undone, my health was severely in crisis, and as a result I made the decision to have a hysterectomy. A huge year to say the least. Three days after the hysterectomy operation, I was in serious trouble and was rushed to emergency theatre for a four-hour operation. I ended up in intensive care unit fighting for my life, as my bowel had been perforated. While I was in ICU all I could think about was all the things I had said I was going to do and never had. Was my eighteen-year-old daughter going to be without a mother? Although

> *"Continuous learning is critical to sustaining and building a business"*

I pulled through and was released weeks later, I now had to contend with a colostomy bag, medical tubes, a stomach that looked worse than Frankenstein's face, and little ability to work for some time. This wiped me out financially, energetically, and spiritually. I remember wondering how on earth do I pick myself up from this one, what was the positives from this disaster? I began listening to Anthony Robbins on my iPhone "Every day in every way I am healthier and healthier or stronger and stronger." With this I found my confidence, positive mind set and voice again.

I took a year off in total to heal, and to learn new skills. My business and I now have a whole new brand. My business is now rocking My new mantra became 'Life is too short to waste, you never know what is going to happen in the next minute, week, month, or year, so make everything you do count and do whatever it is that gives you your joy juice!"

Time away from my business, healing and learning, was actually a blessing in disguise. I realised that many more individuals and organisations around the globe really valued the Feng Shui way. I am now building a global presence and I also love to answer what was once a dreaded question. "Is this a real business?" You bet it is!

Sharon Brown

www.globalpalaceoffengshui.com.au

Sharron Attwood

Brand etiquette for better business

*"We do not see things as they are –
we see them as we are."*

-Anaïs Nin

Sharron has always been a willing ambassador for every school she's attended, company she's worked for, or community group she's joined. Some of her proudest moments have been as a chosen representative of her peers or employers.

But after spending more than ten years at her first job, she was made redundant at the company she had been so dedicated to. She'd attached much of her identity and brand to theirs and now felt at a loss. So started her quest to find out who she really was and what she was capable of doing.

Sharron has worked in corporate, government, small business, and been self-employed. She's studied at university, TAFE, community colleges, private colleges, and online, across a broad range of topics including business, health science, NLP, beauty therapy, sales, art, styling, and public speaking. She utilises much of what she's learned in her metaphorical toolbox. Hindsight has shown her that every experience has a purpose, and you should never see anything as a waste of time—you either earn or you learn.

As a lifelong learner of personal development methodologies, Sharron threw herself into this field of study on a massive scale. She enjoyed learning about herself, but when that started feeling too self-indulgent it evolved into a business. She started working as a life coach and still enjoys coaching as part of her business now. She was soon invited to speak at meetings of her peers—on first impressions, on networking, and on confidence. She still couldn't see the niche evolving. It took a couple of mentors and some well-meaning colleagues to point out the obvious . . .

Sharron has a passion for helping people to achieve greater clarity around their personal brand—inside and out—and to ensure they have the mindset in place to put the best version of themselves out in the world.

Have you always wanted to own your own business?

Not at all.

Growing up I had known people to 'lose everything' being self-employed. It sounded harder than a job—more stress and no one to tell you if you were doing things right. Of course I now know that true wealth is what you have after all the money is gone—but that moment of clarity came twenty-five years later!

I joined one of the big four banks straight out of high school. My hard-working, conservative parents were very proud and it was the kind of job everyone approved of. I loved the uniform, the scarves, and the name badges. I'd always been a bit of a people pleaser, so it sat well with me. I flourished in the bank—attending university at their suggestion and steadily rising through the ranks to work at their state office. Then after ten amazing years my position was moved to Melbourne—and I didn't. I accepted redundancy and realised I didn't have a title any more. I was beholden to the job ads in Saturday's paper.

I needed the same rush of contribution that my corporate job had allowed me—but on my terms.

I went on to work in recruitment, government training, telecommunications, and in the beauty industry—all the while I was working on my own personal development.

My husband has owned his own business for twenty years, and as the business expanded, I wanted to contribute. I worked with him in what was then 'our' business. Except it wasn't. I could see what I wanted to do now though—how I wanted to be of value. I'd develop my ideas and have the flexibility I needed to step out on my own. I undertook a diploma of Life Coaching, NLP training, and a raft of other courses, developing my own business and a commitment to continuing education.

I still happily contribute to the family business and whilst I'm sure my husband was sorry to lose the best employee he ever had—my family supports the path I am on. I couldn't imagine contributing at this level any other way.

How do you stay inspired and motivated?

Have the end in mind. I have a big hairy audacious goal for the future of my business and I know how that will impact me and my family. It excites me. The challenges are less challenging when they form part of a bigger, more exciting picture. When we have momentum we can keep on moving on.

Have a buddy. I have worked with many coaches over the years that have helped me set my goals and work through challenges. Yes—coaches have coaches. It can be inspiring to share your journey when you find someone who 'gets you.' I have no issue coming off as a little crazy, but having a mentor confirm I'm not completely bonkers is welcomed feedback!

> *"Working with someone just starting to dip their toe into the pool of their own magnificence is awesome!"*

Love what you do. I honestly love working with clients and networking with my peers. People inspire me: people on the move, people with vision, people who know there is more out there and are taking steps to have more, be more, do more. I value being able to contribute to the journey of another.

That said, working with someone just starting to dip their toe into the pool of their own magnificence is awesome!

Top up your tank. I read all the time, for education and motivation. Blogs, books, and articles are everywhere. I also love personal development CDs and make use of time spent driving listening to them. I've listened to *Awaken the Giant Within* over a hundred times in the car, yet every time I hear just what I need to hear— sometimes for the first time. Even music can be motivational. I plan out a soundtrack for success when I'm on the way to an event, ensuring I arrive with the required energy level, whether it's calmed by classical music or pumped up by 80s rock.

Have an outlet. I need to share what I am learning, which motivates me to work with others and to speak out. Similarly, I am motivated to keep learning so that I always have the latest or most relevant information to share.

Choose awesome! Choose your standards—keep them high and get your mindset right so you are effortlessly motivated. It needs to be an inside job for long-term success. I'll bet there are loads of ways you inspire others so why not inspire yourself!

What is your view on personal and professional development?

It is not negotiable. I love that there is always something to learn. It stands to reason that for my clients to invest in me, I must always be investing in myself.

Personal development impacts and improves all aspects of my life. I am a firm believer that to know it you have to share and teach it. I always aim to share the content of a new learning within twenty-four hours. It's a way to pay it forward – whilst grounding the training in my brain. We learn more than we realise; how often do you emerge from a course, or even finish reading a book, and feel unsure that it has sunk in? By sharing the content you realise how much of it you took in.

Anything that will strengthen your skills and allow you to put the best version of you out there is vital, be it in business or life in general. Clear your mind of concern and seek out support to develop your personal skill set, whether it's through a course with a tangible outcome or something that tests you and brings out a quality you never realised you had.

If you had to do it all over again, is there anything you would do differently?

YES! I would follow advice and not try to reinvent the wheel. I would have started sooner so I could fail earlier and make the necessary corrections.

As they say, a ship in the harbour is safe, but that is not what ships are built for! I played a small game too long, too safe, too concerned with judgment. I felt I needed more training or more experience in order to be of use.

I now realise that I only have to be one step ahead to help another on their journey, by offering a different view or a reframe.

I would have also built my networks earlier and more efficiently. Strategic networking—meeting with your peers with purpose—has had a tremendous effect on me and my business. You could spend all day every day at events and seminars if you so desired—which is why I've made the distinction around 'strategic networking.' I go where there is mutual value. I need to be able to contribute. In the beginning, though, go everywhere; then work out where you can make a contribution.

How do you juggle your work/life balance?

When I think about this work/life balance thing, I cringe a little. Is it really as hard as we think or are we just conditioned by the reams of articles, tons of books, and plethora of courses on the topic to think it should be?

I refuse to justify the way I balance things. I may get judged but I don't let it affect me. It's just feedback. I've had many hours of coaching around it though, and I'd recommend you do the same if a fear of being judged consumes you. No one knows me, my family and our needs the way we do.

I often feel like the circus acrobat balancing the plates as they spin atop the sticks, needing to keep everything moving. We can learn from the acrobat though—they watch everything with a sense of expanded awareness and monitor the needs of each plate.

I keep a meticulous diary to monitor my 'plates,' and I schedule everything—even time to think about things! I work back from deadlines and note when to start a project. I meet with my husband to discuss the following week, then issue him with reminders at three days prior, forty-eight hours prior, and the day of him needing to pick the kids up or attend something. But it gets done. I also love lists – from to-do lists to shopping lists. Crossing things off the list makes me feel supremely powerful! I learned a long time ago to set a to-do list the night before. Not right before bed, but to have it ready so you can start achieving as soon as you wake up.

> "It's a matter of priorities and how we choose to invest the time we have. Everything is a choice."

It's never an issue of time or in particular 'not enough time.' It's a matter of priorities and how we choose to invest the time we have. Everything is a choice. People have achieved more than me with less time than I have.

I now have dedicated working hours and dedicated family time. At times they cross-over and I'll call a client while the kids do homework or attend dance or sport. Similarly I'll attend a school meeting on a 'work' day.

That's life—that's the balance.

What type of education do you value?

All types have value, and I will defend that opinion with my last breath.

Anything that teaches us something or changes us in some way I would consider education. I value my time at university as much as I value a conversation with a stranger whilst waiting for a bus, if that conversation causes me to flex my mind and think.

Formal education delivers on content and fulfils a requirement.

There is value in going to school and just learning to learn—to know it's possible. There is value in acquiring the knowledge required to follow your passion at a high level. I applaud those who can commit to a path of formal tertiary education, so long as you are open to change. It's ok to change direction—nothing is wasted. It's just another arrow in your quiver.

We can't rely on the school of hard knocks for everything.

Education for personal interest allows us to try new things. I once took oil painting classes at night school with my sister. We learned that we were not very talented at oil painting, but more than that, we learned how much fun it was to show up and give it a go.

Working with people and being with my kids is my favourite kind of education. I learn about them and about myself. You cannot interact with another person and remain unchanged.

Is speaking a part of your marketing strategy?

Those who know me would tell you that speaking is a part of my 'everything' strategy. I'm on a mission.

I started public speaking formally in high school. I loved it as a means of communicating and as a craft. It was a way, and still is, to

> "There is value in acquiring the knowledge required to follow your passion at a high level."

get across the passion I have for my story and for the content I have to share with the like-minded as well as the 'merely interested.'

As a keynote presenter, workshop facilitator, and panellist, I've had the opportunity to speak with many more people than I would ever have the chance to one-on-one. So as a marketing strategy it's a very effective way of getting my message out—of letting people experience me and my brand. They can then choose to work with me if my message, my passion, my way of getting things done, resonates with them and where they are at in their journey.

I've had way more people want to work with me because they 'feel' we can achieve together, as opposed to just being impressed by all the training I have done and awards won. I'm sure the latter gives them some peace of mind, but qualifications alone will not support you in the personal development industry.

What have been some of your most difficult challenges in business?

Setting my prices was very difficult. We might call it an 'investment' and refer to it as 'value' but at the end of the day you need to ask for money. It's not a case of comparing apples with apples in my industry. No one is out there offering the same product as me as 'they' aren't 'me.' No one has the same skill set I offer, with the same outcomes I provide.

My clients value themselves and see a benefit in their lives and their business in working with me. If a prospect can't see the value in working with me then either I'm not the right fit for them, or I haven't shown sufficient value to them.

In a personal sense, I was challenged by the concern that I couldn't deliver enough value or create enough change to meet the expectations of my clients.

Even when I met or exceeded their expectations I'd feel they should have expected more. I guess that this is the tap on the shoulder that drives me to do the very best I can do with every client or organisation I work with. Give them my very best.

That is who I am and that is what my brand is all about.

Sharron Attwood

www.sharronattwood.com.au

Sue Papadoulis

Journalist & Publicity Expert

"When you follow your bliss . . .
doors will open where you would
not have thought there would be
doors, and where there wouldn't
be a door for anyone else."

-Joseph Campbell

For ten years, Sue worked as a journalist and news editor in Australia and London. Yet during a major *aha* moment, Sue realised journalism was no longer the right field for her, and so she made the decision to move into one of the only other career options available: public relations. She hoped to shed the jadedness she'd picked up after a decade of reporting shocking and disturbing stories. Yet she did not feel she truly belonged in the frothy, bubbly world of PR, either.

After getting married and having a baby, Sue decided to start her own PR agency from her home. Despite generating millions of dollars of free publicity for her clients, though, it still wasn't enough. She wanted to inspire others to step up, reach higher, and play a bigger game.

She realised she could easily and effectively teach entrepreneurs how to do their own PR work and get great results. And so, her seminars and trainings began.

Sue has also had the privilege of co-authoring two inspiring books: the Amazon bestseller *Align, Expand, and Succeed: Shifting the Paradigms of Entrepreneurial Success*, and *Ignite Your Business Mojo*.

She has managed to turn her experience of the media from one that was largely negative, into a force for good—not just for herself, but for so many others.

Have you always wanted to own your own business?

No, it was never really a dream of mine! The only reason I started my own business was out of fear.

I had just had our first baby and was on maternity leave from my government job in public relations. I realised pretty quickly that I would need to earn an income but I was terrified of the idea of putting our baby into day-care and going back to this job I no longer enjoyed. The only thing that terrified me slightly less was starting a business. It was a real 'step off the cliff' moment.

> *"I'm very focussed on ensuring I set my day up for success. Project work always gets a block of time each day in the diary that doesn't get changed."*

I launched my first business as a PR consultant when our daughter was five months old. Within six months I'd generated a six-figure income and have never looked back. I've run three businesses in the last eight years, culminating in Publicity for Profit, which is now a national, million-dollar business.

There was always a feeling that I could make my own destiny in some way. I chose journalism as a profession because I was excited by the possibility of writing for a living. Interestingly, I held the belief that choosing my passion meant not earning particularly good money, which was a sacrifice I was willing to make in the short-term.

I can see now that my career as a journalist and then as a public relations executive was preparing me to create Publicity for Profit where we help entrepreneurs get free publicity in the media.

What does a typical day look like to you?

My day starts early. I often rise around 5am and work for an hour when the house is quiet and my creativity is at its peak. At this time I'm only focussed on project work designed to grow the business. I don't open emails or get caught up in anyone else's agenda.

I exercise four or five times a week and this is done at the gym at 6am. My husband and I share school drop-off and pick-up, so I'm either doing the school run until 9.30am or at my desk at 8.30am.

Once I'm at my desk I look for an uncomfortable thing to do that I might otherwise put off. I complete one of those tasks before opening emails, where I'll respond to anything urgent, and then getting back to project work.

I'm very focussed on ensuring I set my day up for success. Project work always gets a block of time each day in the diary that doesn't get changed. I rarely have meetings that aren't 100% necessary because attending one meeting outside the office can wipe out half a day. I prefer phone meetings or face-to-face on Skype. When I do have meetings they're usually in the afternoon when my energy is at its lowest. This is also when I'll return phone calls.

Once a week I have two hours set aside for errands—that's for myself or the household, otherwise life gets out of balance quickly and I start to feel like all I ever do is work. I have fun with this and look forward to it. It could be things like creating a family photo book of our summer, or researching a holiday or even new household appliance.

I'm also a firm believer in outsourcing, especially if you're working full-time. My husband runs his own business and between us we have four children, so it's busy! For that reason, we outsource all kinds of things—house-cleaning, gardening, car detailing, plus we have a housekeeper who comes once a week to do washing, ironing, and cooking. My mother, who has always been a proud housewife, can't quite believe it, but it works for us.

Have you had many mentors on your journey?

I have had a few select mentors who have been pivotal in the success of my business. It's absolutely important to have mentors but it's equally important not to follow the latest shiny object. In my business I see a lot of people who've done numerous courses from various mentors and are probably more confused than when they started.

> "It's absolutely important to have mentors but it's equally important not to follow the latest shiny object."

Taking on a mentor is best when it's done strategically. The smart way to go about it is to create a plan of the expertise you could benefit from in the business, and then research who is the best person to assist.

I also believe choosing someone who is an expert in their area is a better option than looking for an 'all-rounder.' If you feel you need help with accounting and finances, find someone who specialises in that. If you feel your issue is more around a lack of marketing or promotion, find an expert in that.

In the last five years since starting Publicity for Profit, I've employed mentors in the areas of business systems, cash flow management, bringing technology into our business, speaking from stage, online marketing, and most recently, mindset and personal performance.

What are some of your business fears?

Fear is a favourite topic of mine and I regularly speak about it. One of the things I've accomplished well in the last five years is moving through fear and limiting beliefs.

When we start out we all have fears such as 'Is this going to work?' 'I'm not like everyone else, so this probably won't work for me,' 'Do I really know what I'm talking about?' 'Who would ever want to hire me?' 'Is what I know and do valuable to anyone?'

Once you get a few early runs on the board in business those kinds of fears dissipate, but they're replaced by bigger fears, such as 'I'm never going to earn enough money' 'What if I don't get that contract/new client and I can't pay my bills?' 'I can't do this as well as everyone else,' 'I'm scared of being around successful and intimidating people.'

I've encountered all of those fears and plenty more. What I've realised is that moving through fear is simply a part of the process of running a business. Each time I've moved through a fear, my turnover increases and business grows.

I had the good fortune of deciding to move through one of the biggest fears about five years ago. This fear prevented me from doing what I wanted to do for much of my twenty-year career in the media. It stopped me from going for promotions and applying for jobs I would have loved to do.

The fear that held me back was a massive and crippling fear of public speaking. I now run a business conducting live seminars and trainings and am often invited to speak before audiences of hundreds of people. This is something I could never have imagined just six years ago. If I found a way to get beyond that, then I believe anyone can move through any fear.

The process of moving through the fear was firstly about making the conscious decision to be open to it—that was in fact the most difficult aspect. Then a strategy I used that made a real difference was making decisions from where I wanted to be. I pretended my limiting belief around speaking didn't exist. I got into the habit of making a firm and fast decision when I felt the 'yes' inside me. And the final thing was to take action in the moment. If you feel 'yes' and you don't act to commit in the moment, you're opening a gap where fear can enter and talk you out of doing it. For me, when the invitation to speak finally appeared in an email one day, I responded quickly that I would be happy to take up the opportunity—and in that moment, I was a speaker.

Did you ever feel like giving it all up to get a 'real' job?

No, never. Quite the opposite. I quickly realised that by becoming a business owner, I'd pretty much ruined any chance of me ever going to work for someone else. I'd make the worst employee because I've been running my own show for several years and would find it terribly frustrating not being in the driver's seat.

The comment about a 'real job' is interesting because it comes up for a lot of our clients who are solo entrepreneurs or small business owners. Many of our clients have had people close to them say 'Wouldn't it be easier if you just got a real job?'

This question is often asked by people who have a vested interest in keeping us small. It's not said with malice; it's said out of fear. The people who ask this question are worried we might leave them and they are worried about you staying safe. Being safe often means playing a smaller game because there are inherent risks in running a business. If you have someone in your circle that has a vested interest in keeping you small, be aware of it and be mindful of not taking on their fear as your own.

What are you most proud of in your business?

I'm extraordinarily proud of our clients who achieve amazing results in the media. While we help people get publicity in the media, ultimately their success is up to them, so it requires consistent and persistent action.

We help our clients break through that barrier of fear and limiting beliefs that sees them appearing on national TV shows like *Sunrise* or the *Project*, as

> *"Having a ring-side seat while someone pushes through a personal barrier makes our work a blessing."*

well as capital city newspapers, magazines, radio programs, and online news outlets.

To see the transformation of a business owner from someone who doubted their ability, to then appearing on a high rating TV show, is phenomenal. Having a ring-side seat while someone pushes through a personal barrier makes our work a blessing.

I'm also very proud of our team who are all undergoing their own personal transformations. I'm all about inspiring people to step up and play a bigger game, and that includes our staff. If your staff is not growing themselves then the business quickly becomes stale. We're very fortunate that in the last five years we have only had one staff member leave.

As not all success is planned—do you have any accidental success stories?

You could say that my entire business was an accidental success.

The idea of giving small- to medium-sized enterprises the skills to get publicity in the media was born out of another business and, to be honest, I wasn't sure it would work. My business coach at the time encouraged me to package up what I knew about getting publicity in the media and create a webinar series, which is where this all began. I had no concept at the time that it would be a multi-million dollar idea!

Of course it then took a lot of hard work and dedication to make the idea a reality and see it through to what we provide today, which is live seminars and trainings, but I doubt very much that I would have come up with the idea myself.

Do clients care about your why and your brand story?

Absolutely! It's probably one of the biggest reasons why your clients become your clients. I have learned this through running hundreds of live seminars. The most positive feedback about the seminar is always about the stories I tell relating to how and why I got started.

I could be sharing some amazing content about how to get publicity, but without fail, it's always the personal stories about 'how' and 'why' that create a synergy and resonance with your clients.

If you can touch people emotionally with your 'why' and your brand story, the sales aspect becomes almost effortless.

Sue Papadoulis
www.publicityforprofit.com.au

Tasha Broomhall

Helping you to BLOOM

"It had long since come to my attention that people of accomplishment rarely sat back and let things happen to them. They went out and happened to things."

-Leonardo da Vinci

Tasha has always had a keen interest in removing the stigma surrounding mental illness. Since 2007, she has been the director and lead facilitator of the workplace mental health consultancy, Blooming Minds. Prior to that, she delivered mental health training to service providers to help them understand the mental health needs of their clients. While she found this work rewarding, she also became concerned when more and more staff that she was teaching would come to her to discuss their own mental health needs. Tasha has worked with clients from diverse cultural backgrounds, age groups, and socio-economic ranges. Tasha continued to feel that mental health issues needed to be destigmatised, so it would not be as scary for people to get the help they needed. Some people had been struggling with these issues for years, doing whatever possible to mask it from others.

Her studies in psychology and disability, followed by working in psychiatric vocational rehabilitation, as well as her own experiences with anxiety and depression, have equipped Tasha with the theory, real-life experience, and practical skills to develop innovative programs to improve organisations mental health literacy.

Not long after her second child was born, the idea for Blooming Minds started to come to fruition as well. Tasha was asked to fill in as a presenter at a conference when a former co-worker was unable to. Though she had spoken at conferences before, Tasha found this experience to be somewhat different. Yes, she was presenting for the company she used to work for, but at the same time, she was doing it independently. This experience gave her a bit of insight into just what it might feel like were she to branch out on her own and be her own boss. Her business has now grown to include four principle staff, and, in 2014, Tasha published her first book "Bloom! Mental Health & Wellbeing," which was listed in SANE Australia's Top 5 mental health books of 2014 (nominated by the public) and Blooming Minds was awarded the 2014 Private Sector Award for Suicide Prevention Initiatives in workplaces.

Have you always wanted to own your own business?

From a young age I knew that I would own my business, and although the type of business changed over the years, my interests always involved serving others in some way. When I was in primary school (a few years ago now!) I wanted to be a doctor with my own practice. Then one day a friend cut herself while playing at my house and asked me to sit with her while the doctor stitched it up. Just as he was putting the first stitch in, I fainted! I realised I didn't much like the sight of blood and decided I would be a lawyer instead. That idea faded and I wanted to be a clinical psychologist. But it was always going to be my own business.

There is a spattering of solopreneurs in my family but none with much success, so I don't think I consciously wanted to follow in any footsteps. Being able to set up a business in my way, around my values and interests is what I love most about the company I have established. I get to determine which way the business heads and what projects I wish to focus on. It is a fabulous way to work.

What does a typical week look like to you?

Generally my weekdays divide into office days, presenting days, and Oscar days. Usually there are two days of research—course or product development and my own professional development; two days present-ing courses or at conferences; and a day off to spend with my children (Oscar who is one and Maisy and Matilda who are at school). I then work one to two evenings during the week to make up the extra work from my Oscar day. While I still have a young child at home I find this a perfect balance for me. I get a full week's work done, flexibly around my family and personal commitments.

Some weeks see me working with executives, other weeks I'm with trades' people. I find the diversity of groups that we work with keeps me energised and interested. Even if I deliver the same program with four different groups, it is different each time. They will have different goals, different reasons for being in the course, different personal expe-riences, biases, and beliefs. This provides a lot of variety for me in terms of the research and development I need to do for each group and allows me to learn so much from others' experiences.

What advice would you give to someone thinking about starting their own business?

I have five things I suggest for someone wanting to start their own busi-ness:

1) Start before you're ready. Don't wait until everything is perfect or you will never get started. Do your due diligence, research the viability of your product or service as a business idea and ensure you really do have the expertise to be doing what you say you can. Then get started. If it's important to you then get started now. You don't need a concrete brand to start. This can evolve. I've had many people tell me they can't get started until they get their website/business cards/professional photos/flyers printed. You

can get started, if you start with a clear idea of:

- o WHY are you doing it? What do you want to achieve and how do you wish to serve others? Starting with your WHY and understanding your own motivation is important. This needs to be broader than financial goals. Because you will likely face tough times in any business (especially at start up or expansion periods) where your financial goals are not being realised and if this is the only WHY you have then you may give up. If your purpose is bigger it can sustain you through the tougher times. Your WHY also acts as a rudder to keep you on course when shiny stars of new opportunities or ideas come shooting past. If it doesn't serve your WHY then don't chase it.

- o WHAT unique product or service can you provide that will achieve this? What is unique or different about your approach? Where is there a gap in the market that you can serve? Understanding your point of difference from the outset is important. There will always be new businesses that come along to serve your market, especially when you are doing well and others want to jump on board, so knowing what you can uniquely offer and then owning that space is a great way to start and to be sustainable.

- o WORK from your values. If you know what your business values are and allow this to shape any actions you take, decisions will be simpler and you will be more comfortable with the direction your business takes. If your business is not aligned with your values, the level of dissonance can be paralysing and you may no longer want to be in your business. Don't compromise your values for a quick win;

keeping aligned with your values may at times be a slower road, however, it is a more authentic and purpose-driven one.

2) Get a professional mentor (or two!), someone who has trod the boards you wish to follow and can help you to stay steady when times are tricky (because these times will come). They are someone to bounce ideas off and to give you their wealth of experience. You may need a few different mentors with different skill sets and availability, depending on the complexity of your business goals. That's ok; there is no quota that says you can only have one. Finding a mentor is an active process. Think about who you think would be an ideal mentor for you and then don't be shy to ask! However, don't be disheartened if they say no. The timing may not be right for them; they may have other commitments that are pressing, they may be going through a stage of growth themselves and want to focus on their own needs. It's much better for them to say no if they are not able to commit to mentoring you, rather than say that they will and then not being accessible because they are too busy. Treat your mentor well. You be the one who pays for lunch or coffee when you meet up and be punctual and prepared for any sessions, so you are not wasting their time.

The day will come when you are asked to be the mentor. Approach this humbly with respect for the mentee. If you have the time and interest to work with them, do so with generosity of your experience. I have been so blessed with having two longstanding mentors who have guided and supported me and I now have the awesome honour to provide mentoring for others. It is such a brilliant opportunity to support someone who is forging their own path. I do this freely with a spirit of reciprocity to pass forward the generosity of what has been freely provided to me.

3) Don't try to convince clients they should work with you. Look for those who already know they need your service and show them how you can assist.

4) Don't get into cost-cutting. Do a thorough assessment of your business costs and revenue and cost your services or products appropriately. If you are charging a price that you believe you can give value for then stick with it. Don't get into the space of charging less and less because there will always be others who go for the quick sale and undercut you on price. However time may prove they also undercut on quality. If a client genuinely can't afford your service then work with them on what areas of your service could you omit to get closer to their budget? There may be elements that you offer that at times are not as relevant to their needs, but don't get into a scarcity mindset driven cost-cutting frenzy. Stand by the value of what you deliver if it's aligned with your business WHY and your business values.

5) Don't be desperate. I have heard people speak very inappropriately about competitors and to take unethical steps such as presenting another person's material/information/copying service offerings/advertising, etc, and the problem is it's actually selling yourself short. Yes sometimes you'll get away with it, but if you're not good enough to come up with your own material/own services/own value for clients, then what are you doing in that business in the first place?

How critical is it to have a team to support you?

Very critical if you want to grow your business. Ernesto Sirolli talks about how businesses have three core needs: someone to design or deliver the product/service; someone to market or sell it; someone to look after the money. In his vast global experience of working with entrepreneurs he says he's never found one person who can play all three roles in a business. And I'd add that even if you do have skills in all three areas, as your business grows, do you really have time to do all three roles or could your business goals be better served by delegating and outsourcing? You need to ensure that your staff understand and support your brand and know how to maintain it.

At Blooming Minds, part of our branding is our expertise. We have developed our brand to ensure that we are different in that the vast majority of participants report that they enjoy our sessions much more than they thought they would and engage with us after the session through our online membership site which offers refreshers of the information covered. It also gives them a chance to stay in touch for consulting to help apply what they've learned. This vastly increases the opportunities for behavioural integration. There is no way an individual could fulfil all of these roles. To be able to offer a dynamic and responsive service to clients before, during and after our education sessions requires a team of dedicated and skilled professionals. Plus it makes our wins so much more fun when we get to share them as a team rather than me fist-pumping myself all alone at my desk!

What drives you on a day-to day-basis?

The stories from people we help through our courses. I am very fortunate that I get to do a job I love and that it's making a difference. Two weeks ago I received an email from a lady out of the blue that was in one of my courses last year. She acknowledged that while she was in the course to learn about her responsibilities as a supervisor of other staff, she herself had been living with depression for a long time. She credited the course as saving her life, her relationship, and her job. When we receive emails like this we understand that the course was a catalyst for the person in distress. We are not the ones doing the hard work—they are—we've just given them some space to reflect on what they need to do and the tools to do it. This is our business WHY and it is so awesome to get to deliver on it again and again.

Do you set regular goals?

Yes. I set overall goals for the direction I'm heading in personally and with my business; I set project-based goals (with times attributed to them) and I set shorter-term daily goals which I call intentions. I have developed a resource for my clients to assist with this, a self-reflection journal called 'Live Consciously and Bloom' and I use this myself every day to set my daily intentions. This keeps me on track with my overall goals and my values.

How do you juggle your work/life balance?

My formula for a balanced and purpose driven life is to 'focus your time and your positive attention' in the areas of your life that are aligned with 'your values.' My idea of balance doesn't require you to spend the same amount of time in various roles; rather you make decisions about how you spend time based on your values and to ensure that time is purposeful and deliberate (e.g. not playing on your mobile while having dinner with your family if connecting with your family positively is a value of yours).

This is not always easy to achieve and you may need to develop some skills in self-management and mindset in order to achieve it. I've had to develop a mindset where I understand it doesn't all have to be done by me, as well as developing skills to delegate appropriately (by training staff, by ensuring I articulate tasks clearly, and by then trusting in the work that has been put in and allowing the results to occur) and I've had to change my money mindset so I live in one of abundance rather than scarcity. And through these efforts I have been able to get a much better balance. Not every day is balanced, but across a week I do achieve balance.

What have been some of your most difficult challenges in business?

My biggest challenge has been financial mindset. In three specific ways:

1) Coming from a not–for-profit background, my early actions were to discount everything for clients, as I was worried about their budgets. The lesson about fees was learnt very early on when I had a client negotiate very strongly to get a significantly reduced fee (less than 50% or the original quote) for a service that they said that they really needed yet they had very limited capacity to fund it. I value the work this client does and I wanted to help as I could see how their staff would benefit from the training program we had designed for them. So I agreed to the reduced price even though it would mean

we just broke even on the program and wouldn't receive any profits to help with business overheads. Then a week after the program ended I ran into two of the staff members who were on a wild, end-of-financial year shopping expedition. They advised me that they had thousands of dollars that needed to be spent before EOFY and so were out on a shopping spree purchasing new cutlery, crockery, glassware, and other furnishings, otherwise their budget will be cut for the next year. I was devastated. Not just because the same organisation that was now throwing away cash had negotiated so hard with me and I felt took advantage of my support of their staff's needs but most importantly because this agency provides services to vulnerable members of our society who have very limited luxuries themselves. I was so upset that they hadn't used any excess funds to support the needs of their clients. I readjusted my perspective on fees from here on.

2) Having been very poorly paid in the NFP sector, I wanted to pay employees and consultants highly as I valued the work that they do. Early in my business this resulted in me not drawing a wage myself for six months while I paid an employee a six-figure salary. Not so sustainable. Ethically I want all involved in the business to be renumerated appropriately for their efforts; however, this means two things:

> i. I also need to be renumerated for my efforts or the business won't continue, as I'll have to get a job to pay the bills (my kids like to eat at least every second day!) and

> ii. I need to cost our services out, including all of the

research and development time, follow-up time, and professional development costs for our own staff as well as usual business overheads.

3) The third element of financial mindset I had to relearn was thinking you can save money by doing everything yourself. You can waste a lot of time, energy and money trying to learn things that could be outsourced to a professional. It is worth considering what elements you can outsource or delegate to others.

Tasha Broomhall
www.bloomingminds.com.au

Todd Hutchison

The Corporate Mechanic

*"Success is not final, failure is not fatal:
it is the courage to continue that counts."*

-Winston Churchill

Todd Hutchison was born in Perth, Western Australia. During high school, he worked weekends at a car wreckers where he was surprised to find that he had been employed alongside David and Catherine Birnie— Australia's most notorious mass murderers. Intrigued by how people can have a public persona that hid their real lives, he began a lifelong pursuit of studying human behaviour.

By the age of seventeen, with a passion for business, he was leading five photographic studios. Later, he went into the television industry and worked around the likes of Michael Jackson, Paul McCartney, Sammy Davis Jr, and Sir Bob Geldof. He also began a lifetime of studying, starting at the Conservatorium of Music, later becoming a world champion (grade 2) with the Western Australian Police Pipe Band at the World Pipe-band Championships in Glasgow, Scotland in 1998.

Never having a year off from university or college, he continued his studies in business, engineering, commerce, information technology, coaching, and training, including a MBA and a Master of Commerce. He is now progressing through a Bachelor of Laws.

He held directorships in organisations like Curtin University and Deloitte, until he finally branched out into his own consulting and training business, now called Peopleistic. The business was created by writing down and drawing the connections between his likes, passions, and uniqueness. By examining the dominating connection lines, he created the business of his dreams.

Todd's studies of behavioural profiling paid off, as he discovered that his barrier to growing a global business was linked to his own genetic fear sensitivities that unduly influence our thinking. When he realised that his style was guided by a need for control and a concern for being taken advantage of, he hit the jackpot—this had made him resistant to having business partners. After that insight, his company grew to an international firm, with other businesses in training, and video production.

His developed talent in strategy, governance, and project management-based consulting led to him being named the *Corporate Mechanic*, and formal recognition as a certified speaking professional by National Speakers Association of Australia, a pre-eminent business leader by WA Business News, a 2013 Worldwide Who's Who Hall of Fame recipient, and the 2014 Global 101 authority in project management.

Today, as an international bestselling author, Todd resides on global company boards and continues to enjoy a life of consulting, coaching, and speaking, as well as family time with his wife, Gina, and daughter, Lara.

What branding advice would you give to someone thinking about starting their own business?

Business helps generate income and touch the lives of those you serve, and they also create an asset that may generate income from its sale or through licensing of its services and products. These are all important factors when considering the brand of your business.

In starting my first business and being a professional speaker, I had to make a key decision on whether the trade name would reflect my personal name, or be separate from me and follow a more traditional company brand pathway. As a speaker, using your own name is a great way to have a consistent branding message of who you are that reinforces your personal brand to a client. After all, you are the brand, and the brand is you. Some names are more memorable than others, and many actors have changed their name for this very reason.

The challenge in using your name is that the business may be less sellable, or it may be more difficult to attract business partners or employees that do not want to work for a brand that markets someone else other than themselves. Remember that the most important person in the world is you, and therefore when you work for a business that has someone else's name, it may make you feel less important, particularly if the name is not already globally known. Traditionally, law and accounting firms have included the founder's surnames, though they are often changed over time as partners come and go.

Some very successful speakers have been able to achieve licensing under their own name, from Brian Tracy's business training programs, and Anthony Robbins's business results coaching programs. You may notice that they first created a global awareness of their name before they went into licensing. These two businesses may be sellable—such as their predecessor mentor, the late Jim Rohn—due to the amount of sellable product they have created that will sell far past their own lifetime. My belief is that your personal name is connected to your reputation, and you want to protect that.

For me, it was an easier decision as I was first and foremost a consultant who spoke as a means of marketing. I was a professional speaker who used speaking as a funnel into gaining consulting and training work for my businesses. It is important that the brand was my company and not me.

I chose to go down this route where the trade name was a business name, and that ultimately attracted other professional speakers and authors across the globe to become business partners and work under the same *Peopleistic* brand globally. This was the trade name for building an international business. It would not have happened if the business included my own name.

How important is it to have a distinctive brand?

Peopleistic actually started as *People Rich*, with the *Rich* representing the enrichment of people's lives. It met all the right marketing elements of being short, unique, and memorable, but it also came with some challenges that became apparent after ten years in business. The word *rich* often gets blocked by email spam filters, and many people have psychological issues with money and therefore the word *rich*. Some people even associated us with wealth creators or financial planners and that was not the brand connection we wanted.

Given the potential negative connotations, we did not want any negativity associated with our brand. It was time to change.

We were all about people, as we recognised that business success was all about people, and the issues we were addressing at the end of the day for our clients were actual people issues. We understood that even systems and processes existed to guide behaviour, so whether you were dealing in strategy, process, or team development, the common element was people. We sensed that keeping the word *people* in our brand was paramount.

Your brand needs to feel right for you, reflect your values, and be something you are proud to be connected with. The companies that have done it well attract brilliant people as the brand has created goodwill—it means something to people.

Although having established offices in Australia, the United States, and the United Kingdom, we took the bold move to rebrand. Each chief executive officer in our global business was about to become co-authors in a new *Humanistic Business* book through the publisher Bloomsbury, which was the centre theme of our new business model, and it was a timely change.

The challenge was in finding a name that was unique enough to have all the Internet domain names available in every country we operated, as well as the availability of the trade name to secure it as a business name. We agreed that the brand *People Intel* well represented who we were: a company that specialises in the people

> "*A good technique in developing a brand name is to tell the market what you do in your name.*"

intelligence discipline. Unfortunately, that soon attracted legal letters on behalf of the large corporation using a similar name.

We had not marketed the new name, and on legal advice, we elected to change to a different brand name before progressing any further. Strangely, registering a trade name had not caught their attention, so we had assumed that a company name change would be safe. We were wrong. Keeping the *people* in the name was important to us and we were already known in the market as People Rich. We also had a lot of video content that had vertical banners in the background that we could continue using if only we found a good second half to the brand name.

It was one of our team members who had the bright spark to link it to our new business model and new book that was branded *Humanistic Business*. That was it: *Peopleistic*. It was short, unique, catchy, included the word people in it, and made for a single word. Many successful companies make up a brand name, and the inclusion -*istic* had the meaning of being connected to, or representative of, so it made total sense.

We secured the domain names, and we undertook a global transition to the new and exciting Peopleistic brand. We also updated our aged logo as part of the rebranding activity. It has really worked, as feedback has been positive, and it is memorable. It was an easy transition from our former name, as most people at least remembered that our business name started with People. When clients' searched on the Internet for us, they inevitably remember both the first name and the first word of the business name, if not all of it. So we hit the jackpot!

How important is positioning in the market place?

Our sister company, formerly known as the *Australasian College of Leadership and Coaching* was an Australian government approved registered training organisation and is a great example of using the branding in positioning in the marketplace. It started with a focus on coaching education.

We had also recognised the limits in its name as our main programs ended up being in project management (making things happen). Projects represent where strategy meets execution, and whilst we saw the link to leadership, the market may have been confused. We needed a broader name, as our focus on coaching and leadership development was expanding.

A good technique in developing a brand name is to tell the market what you do in your name. That was the principle we took in rebranding to the *Business Education Institute*. It tells you that we are an educational entity with a focus on business-related training.

Our separate company's logos have stayed true to our original brand colours of purple and gold. Colours have known psychological meanings. Purple represents leadership, a sense of power and authority, steadiness and strength, with a link to spirituality. Gold represents success, happiness, optimism, and enlightenment. Both reflected our desired positioning.

When did you know your story could be a brand?

Sometimes it is not so much your story, it is what you do or are known for, which automatically presents the opportunity for a brand. I had recognised that there were complications with people remembering your personal name or what you did. My surname, Hutchison, was often misspelled *Hutchinson*, so people may not have found me so easy on an Internet search. As a speaker, being able to be found online is important, and I work on the principle to be easy to do business with. Being hard to find is against this principle. I definitely was known for certain services in different marketplaces due to my wide and diverse personal interests, but my common theme was making a difference in "fixing" things in the corporate environment.

The name *Corporate Mechanic* came to be after I did a profile tool that suggested I had *mechanic* profile style. The name felt right; it gave you enough insight about what I did and what market I played in. I became known as Todd Hutchison, the Corporate Mechanic at Peopleistic. I registered the trademark to protect the name, and use it in my introductions going on stage, and in publications. I have found it to be memorable, and have heard many people say, 'You're that corporate mechanic guy.' It has clearly worked.

So in looking at the future, *Peopleistic* and the *Business Education Institute* (and other businesses we now own) are sellable entities that are not connected directly to my name in their brands, but the *Corpo-*

> *"I have found from working around the world that often it is better to run your own business after you have developed experience in other people's businesses first."*

rate Mechanic is a personal brand that works in my speaking, consulting, training, and company director roles. It is like having a personal tagline and they are not the type of things you share. Their purpose is to represent you, as there are others in the world with the same name as you. In fact, I have never been able to own or buy the .com domain as someone else got it first. If your name is available as a domain name—grab it now!

Independent on what people remember, whether it is your personal name, your tagline, or your business name, the important factor is that they remember something that will enable them to find you online. When people do not know what you do, or cannot remember your brand, they cannot refer others to you. Branding I have found is the key to positioning in the busy marketplace.

Have you always wanted to own your own business?

I have found from working around the world that often it is better to run your own business after you have developed experience in other people's businesses first.

I started early in life running businesses others owned. Even back at school, I had found a loophole in the school system that allowed me to go to college at night to study photography while attending school during the day. I had been working on weekends, school holidays, and late night, shopping evenings for a photographic business. By the time I left school I was already effectively qualified and experienced in the photographic business. This ultimately led me to running five photographic studios when the person in charge suddenly left and I was promoted.

I did not want to go out on my own, as I was chasing leadership experience in industries that were based on large corporations. I went into the music and television industry, which was a childhood dream. Along that journey I became qualified in engineering, and so I went into the mainstream engineering environments, working on oil rigs, mine sites, and key research and development operations, as well as large manufacturing plants. I ended up leading the technical services in an engineering school in a university environment, working up to become a director of information technology for their multi-campus operations.

At that point, having had significant leadership experience, business knowledge, and tertiary qualifications to back it up, I started up a part-time business. I took leave to test the business and its market value, and ended up leaving my director role on gaining that proof. I had created a business that made my previous director annual salary within a three-month period. Having been a trouble-shooter and an international consultant working for the likes of Peopleistic and Deloitte globally, you really get exposure to different businesses, and what works.

When you feel you have something special that the market needs, and you have gained the credibility (in the market's eyes) to operate there, you need to at least test it. It will depend on what market you are going for, as my market was more large corporates. It comes down to knowing more about your own strengths and passions, and choosing where you want to play.

Today, having a global business network and multiple complementary businesses, supported by investments in property and shares, I wouldn't work for anyone else. But be prepared that running your own business can be hard work. I have even found I am still enjoying learning, now studying for a Bachelor of Laws. The reality is that we now live in a fast-paced world and need to be life-long learners.

"Knowledge is not power, execution is…
action is where all your power is found"

Anthony Robbins

Todd Hutchison
www.peopleistic.com.au

Veronika Andersson

**The wellness accountant—
caring about you as well
as your finances**

*"There is a language in the world that
everyone understands. The language of
enthusiasm, of things accomplished
with love and purpose, and as
part of a search for something
loved and desired."*

-Paulo Coelho, *The Alchemist*

Veronika spent most of her formative years living in a caravan with her family, travelling around the countryside. It was quite an adventure but money was always tight, despite her father often earning good money. Veronika found herself wondering where it was all going, and it was in part due to this curiosity that she believes she got into accounting.

While holidaying in a caravan was fun for a while, that fun eventually faded, and Veronika found herself highly motivated to seek a better way of life for herself. After she finished high school, she got a job as a trainee in an accounting position.

She has now been working in public practice for more than twenty years. Her favourite part of being an accountant is getting to contribute to the success of the businesspeople she works with. She's gained an enormous amount of knowledge of business structures and business operations and has seen many businesses succeed and grow within the most appropriate structure, management, and teams. She has also seen some fail due to not having these things in place, despite the best of intentions and efforts.

In 2012, Veronika founded Vavee after she noticed a serious lack in the personal contact and servicing of clients by their accountants. The clients were missing out on access to knowledge, information and support, that could help them grow their prosperity exponentially!

Veronika also loves helping start-ups navigate the profit system. Start-ups need to get their structures right the first time around, understand their legal obligations and set realistic financial business goals so they can build and grow a sustainable business.

As a wellness accountant, Veronika looks at the whole picture, beyond the bottom line and the tax result. These are important of course, but she looks a little deeper at what is causing your results. What is working well, what needs adjustment and what needs to be removed completely from your money and business habits? Are there any tools and strategies that could help you reach your long- term goals? These are questions that could make a lasting positive result on your personal and financial success.

Did you come from a family of entrepreneurs?

I grew up with immigrant parents, neither of whom finished primary school and only learned English on the fly after arriving in Australia. Both of them almost literally broke their backs in manual labour jobs all their lives. We travelled the countryside in a caravan and I attended thirteen schools in my first seven years of school. I was not going to be able to get away with that in high school, so I was enrolled in correspondence school and the travel continued.

I was relied upon from a very early age to read and prepare contracts and documents for the family. My father had high expectations of me, and my mother always said I could do anything that I set my mind to, so I did have some belief in myself.

All this travelling was a great adventure and built character and resilience, but it was not producing any wealth for my family. I developed a deep desire to not continue this hand-to-mouth way of life, so it probably was no accident that I kind of fell into accounting, with a traineeship scholarship to study part-time and work full-time for a public practice almost straight out of high school.

My working life was completely foreign to my family. Even though I know they supported me in my work and studies and were very proud of me, they simply could not understand office or university culture.

When I decided to start my own business there was still pride and support, but even less understanding of why I would give up a steady pay check to go into business for myself.

I believe I am a great example that you are not just a product of your environment and you can change your outcomes.

"What we are today comes from our thoughts of yesterday, and our present thoughts build our life of tomorrow: our life is the creation of our mind." -Hindu Prince Guatama Siddhartha, the founder of Buddhism, 563-483BC

Have you always wanted to own your own business?

I worked for other people's accounting practices for over twenty years. I was lucky to be in a position to learn so much from some very experienced and skilled accountants. But the culture was changing. One of my favourite aspects of my job was the client contact, and that was being threatened by structural changes. At the same time I could see that clients' concerns were not being directly addressed and they often had many more questions to ask and no opportunity to ask them in a boardroom meeting environment. Adding even more layers of management was making the situation even worse. Services and client satisfaction was suffering.

I had not intended to start my own practice. But so many other accounting practices that I looked into were heading down the same low service/satisfaction road. And when I spoke to people about their accountants there was a definite tone of dissatisfaction of availability and services provided. There was certainly no education or feedback provided to assist clients in getting better financial results. Luckily I had the support of some clients that I had worked with and managed a very soft landing into my own accounting business. I had a ready-made client base, which was growing organically through word-of-mouth.

Even with this soft start, jumping from an employee mindset to an entrepreneur mindset was a much bigger transition than I anticipated. Sure, I had a pretty good idea how to run an accounting practice. But the regular deposit into my bank account was no longer there. Cash flow was coming in but exactly when was no longer so clear. And there were so many other little tricks to learn in setting up and running a business. This experience has given me a whole new insight into what my clients go through when starting a business. This allows me to give them a little extra support and understanding when required, including waiting patiently and providing pertinent information as people prepare themselves before starting a business.

> *"Try not to be a person of success,*
> *but a person of value."*
>
> -Albert Einstein

Have you had many mentors on your journey?

As I get older, I place more and more importance on being surrounded by positive people, doing great things, and achieving impressive results.

After all, you are the average of the five people that you spend the most time with.

The tools that I have learned from these mentors has helped me identify and address these myself to some extent, so now my focus is on mentors that help me specifically with my business ideas and strategies.

Do you think it is important to have a mentor?

I contrast the results that I have been getting in the past ten years while consciously seeking out mentors, and my results before then. I certainly still appreciate those who supported me or inspired me in some way previously, and I still look back in wonder at how I got so far without mentors. However, becoming conscious of my values and setting goals that satisfied the support of those values has led to some truly amazing people entering my life and creating opportunities that I just could not see before.

Now I know from this experience that it is imperative to find someone who has achieved something similar to what you are aiming for. Even if you just achieve a new perspective, new contacts that can help you along the way, or support from like-minded people.

What is your view on personal and professional development?

Accounting and tax knowledge and expertise are of course vital in the constantly changing Australian tax environment. I consistently exceed accounting body requirements in professional development. And I go beyond accounting and tax. I attend seminars, study and apply a wide range of philosophies in entrepreneurship, business, investment, and also mentorship, presentation, money mindsets, and effective communication.

The library in the office includes authors such as Robert Kiyosaki, Edward De Bono, Napoleon Hill . . . and the list goes on! I have also completed comprehensive trainings both personally and professionally with a range of highly respected providers

Even if I have trained with the same people before or have some background in the subject matter, I approach each training or reading with the attitude 'what else can I learn from this?' I call this a beginner mindset. I find that if I walk into any class or training (for business or even personal such as dance classes!) I come away with a great experience and new tools. I see it happen all the time, where people walk in with an attitude of 'I already know this.' *They are very likely to miss the learning completely,* or at least have a diminished experience or insight. My time and money is too valuable to miss out on anything that potential mentors are willing to pass on to me!

How important is money mindset in business?

One of my very favourite topics! I am fascinated by the emotional charge behind the word 'money.' Some people think it is evil, some believe there is never enough, and some that it causes strain in relationships with loved ones. Listening to people's language can reveal so much about what we believe and the results that we can expect. If I believe money is evil, why would I want to accumulate any?

I deal with the concept of money all day, every day. We all do to some extent. However, I get to see people's relationships with money at a much deeper level.

Money is a very effective tool and nothing more. The more you accumulate, the more good you can do for yourself, your loved ones, and any causes that concern you. The more you accumulate, the more you can contribute.

Money is a tool for measurement. It is how you can measure the success of your business. However, it does not represent your values, or the values that your business provides. Your business goals should be based on your values, and can be measured by reaching monetary targets. An emotional charge behind your values creates motivation. Remove the emotional charge about the tool that is getting you there.

Understanding how to measure and monitor your targets is crucial for business, as well as for wealth creation strategies and even personal finances. I strive to develop products that assist my clients in setting and tracking these targets on all levels.

What have been some of your most difficult challenges in business?

Balance and prioritising, definitely. In my first year in business I believed I could still have all the usual trips away for dance congresses and time for helping out my dance teachers with congresses and classes. (did I mention I love dancing?) And I did. At the time. Then I decided that I had to pull back these activities and focus on my own business. Almost immediately the change in focus was producing exponential growth in my business. Now I just dance for fun and it is a great release from being in the mind all day.

I then went to the other extreme—over a year without any holidays at all. After a week-long yoga retreat in Bali I came back to work with so much energy I finished my first week's work in two days! Yes, finding a balance is a great challenge. Now I schedule in my holidays as well as the work.

The transformation between employee to an entrepreneur was not all smooth sailing, either. The security of regular salary, annual leave, and sick-leave entitlements does not scrape the surface in the change required to the mindset, especially as a solopreneur. Suddenly I was solely responsible for all decisions as well as all the tasks. I will admit that mistakes were made. Again, I have been extremely fortunate to have clients that I have worked with for so long that they stood by me as I had to make this very important mental and emotional transformation. Thankfully I also have some wonderful staff now that I can trust implicitly with supporting my business. The right people are so important.

> *"Every adversity, every failure, every heartache carries with it the seed of an equal or greater benefit."*
>
> -Napolean Hill

Veronika Andersson

www.vavee.com.au

About the Author

Paula has been inspiring audiences for nearly 30 years. Dynamic, infectious, inspiring, commercially savvy, and passionate are all words that have been used by her clients to describe Paula as a presenter, workshop leader, and business coach.

Paula's many roles as a successful business woman/entrepreneur have included director of Australia's largest grooming and deportment school, franchisor, hotel owner, training College director, professional speaker, author, corporate trainer and leadership coach.

From her training rooms to the conference floor, Paula will engage the audience with her energetic spirit, solid expertise, and her unshakeable conviction that a positive mindset leads to an exceptional life. She is the director of the Self Leadership Institute, a boutique training and coaching consultancy helping individuals and organisations to grow their business and their brand.

She is the author of the highly successful books *Speaking in the Shower and Powerful Presentation Principles,* and now *Sell Your Story.* She is recognised as a leading authority on standing up and speaking out.

She has been awarded the CSP (Certified Speaking Professional) designation by the National Speakers Association. Only a small number of professional speakers hold the CSP designation worldwide.

Paula values long-term business relationships and many of her clients have her returning year after year as a partner in meeting their organisational goals.

Paula is also a proud mum of three, wife of one, and friend to a few more. She has been seen attempting the occasional triathlon and enjoys hanging out on her Perth Hills property with her family, close friends, and a whole bunch of adorable alpacas.

www.paulasmith.com.au

Paula Smith – Speaker CSP, Author, Business Consultant, Workshop Leader
(BA Training and Development, Grad Cert Ed, MA NLP)

Made in the USA
Las Vegas, NV
31 August 2023

76900388R00114